topics plus
book 6

Bill Domoney, Paul Harrison, Liz Ransford, Christine Symonds

Nelson

Thomas Nelson and Sons Ltd
Nelson House Mayfield Road
Walton-on-Thames Surrey
KT12 5PL UK

Thomas Nelson Australia
102 Dodds Street
South Melbourne
Victoria 3205 Australia

Nelson Canada
1120 Birchmount Road
Scarborough Ontario
M1K 5G4 Canada

First published by Thomas Nelson and Sons Ltd 1996

I(T)P Thomas Nelson is an International Thomson Publishing Company

I(T)P is used under licence

ISBN 0-17-421975-X (single copies)
ISBN 0-17-421980-6 (pack of 8)
NPN 9 8 7 6 5 4 3 2 1

Acknowledgements

Acquisitions: David McCormick
Project Management: Lesley Wiseman
Editorial: Lynne Williamson
with Maggie Cameron, Marie Lister and Mairi Sutherland
Design: Thumbnail Graphics and StoreyBooks
Production: Susie Home
with Liz Carr and David Lennox

Printed in Great Britain by E. Baylis & Son Ltd, Worcester.

contents

Unit 1 Length

A lengthy business

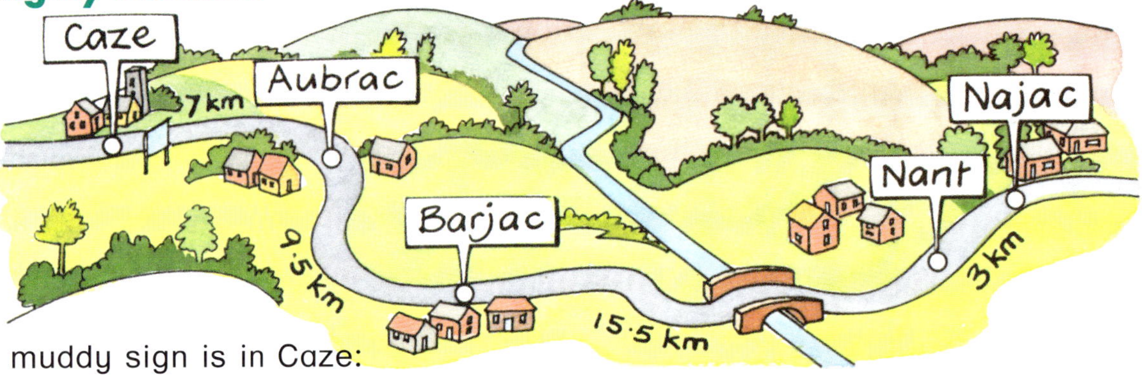

This muddy sign is in Caze:

It is supposed to show the distances to all the other villages.

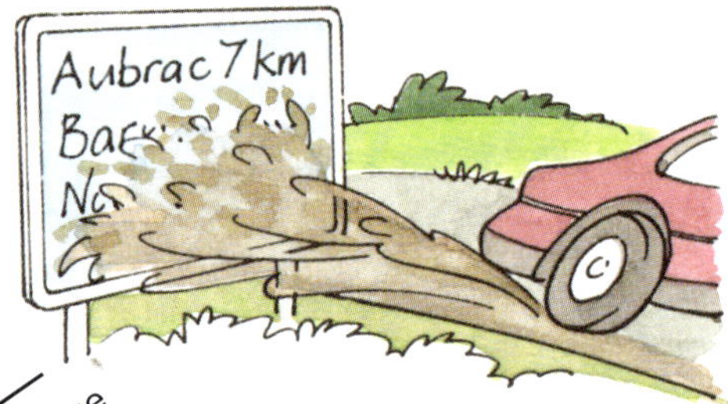

1 Draw the sign with the mud washed off.

2 Copy and complete this distance chart.

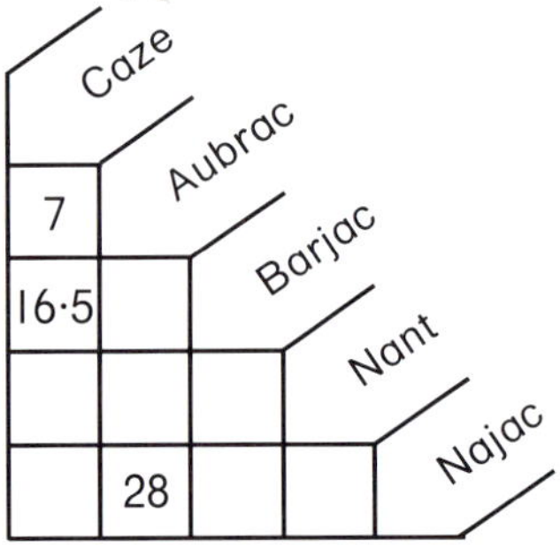

kilometres

Which unit would be best for measuring these: centimetres, metres or kilometres?

3

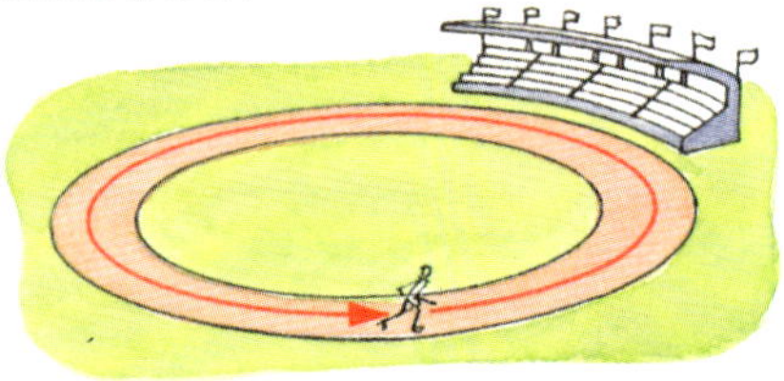

4

5

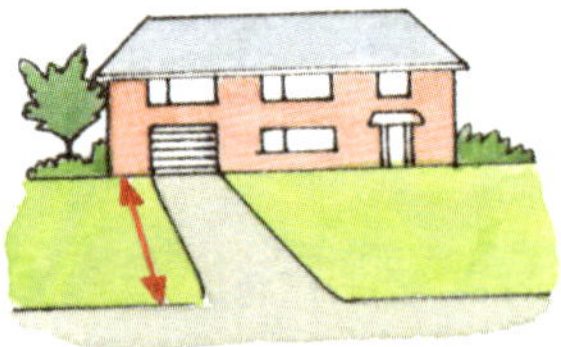

6

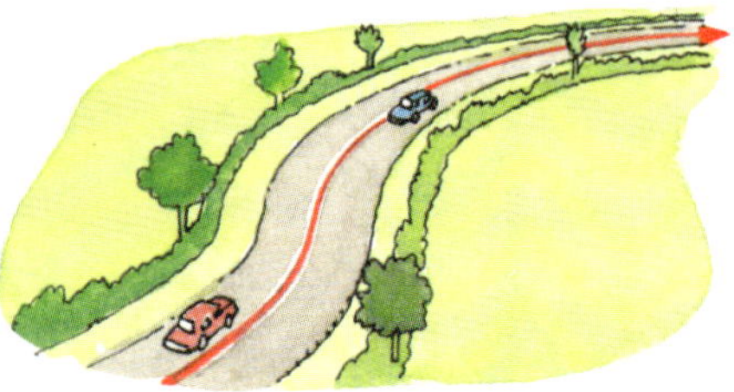

7

8

Making graphs of distances

you need:
5 mm or 1 cm squared paper

This chart shows distances by road between cities.

	Edinburgh	Carlisle	Leeds	Nottingham	Cardiff	Bristol
Carlisle	158					
Leeds	318	195				
Nottingham	425	302	120			
Cardiff	643	483	384	264		
Bristol	610	451	352	232	75	
London	661	501	318	210	248	192

kilometres

What is the distance between these cities **rounded to the nearest 10 km**?

1. Edinburgh and Cardiff
2. Leeds and London
3. Bristol and Carlisle
4. Edinburgh and Nottingham
5. Leeds and Edinburgh via Carlisle
6. Bristol and Carlisle via Nottingham
7. Cardiff and Carlisle via Leeds
8. Which of the cities on the map is nearest to where you live?
9. Write the distances from that city to each of the other cities on the map, rounded to the nearest 10 km.
10. Make a bar graph or a bar-line graph to show the distances from that city to each of the other cities.

Abu lives near London. This is the start of his graph.

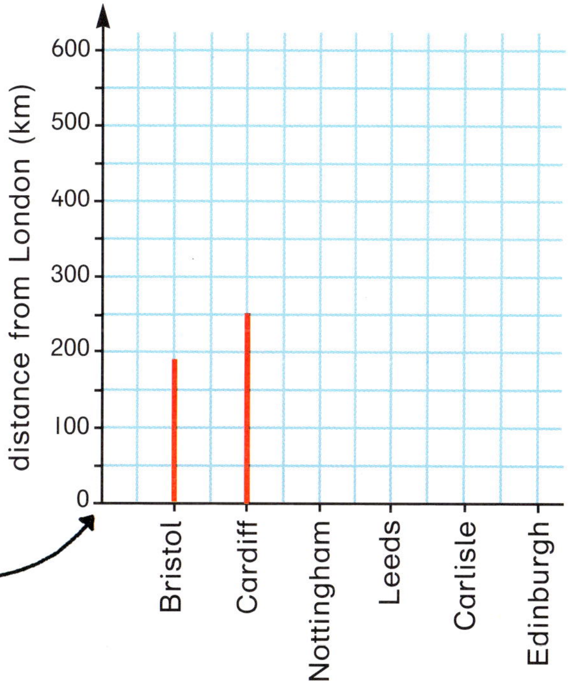

Unit 2 Symmetry

Investigating the symmetry of letters

you need:
large sheet of paper
Multilink cubes

1 Copy the Carroll diagram.

Sort these capital letters into sets according to whether or not they have line symmetry or rotational symmetry. J, O, T and Z are done for you.

A B C D E F G H I J K L M N O P Q R S T U V W X Y Z

	line symmetry	no line symmetry
rotational symmetry	O	Z
no rotational symmetry	T	J

2 Here are some half-finished Multilink models. Use cubes to complete the other half so that they are symmetrical.

you need:

squared paper

scissors

Making patterns with rotational symmetry

Alice wants to colour a pattern on squared paper that has rotational symmetry.

She cuts out an 8 by 8 square and divides it into quarters.

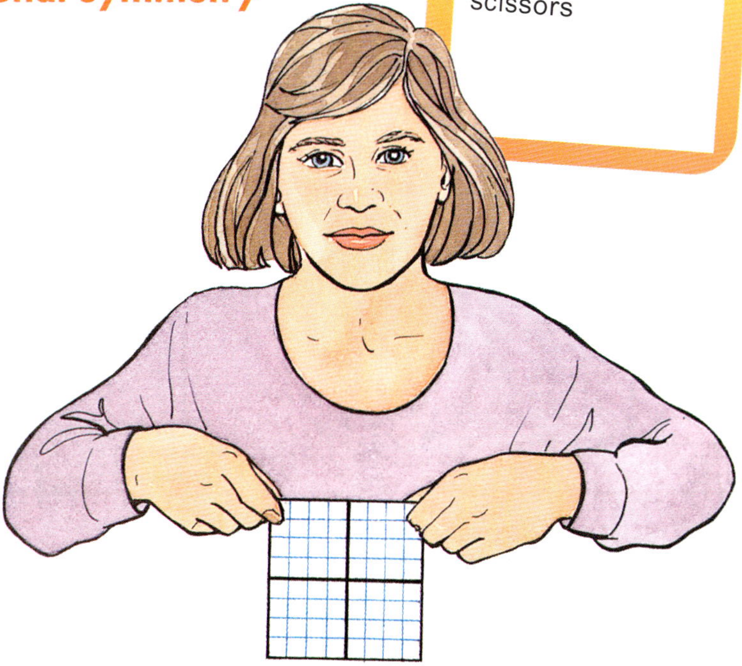

She colours in a pattern in one quarter.

She rotates the paper and colours the same pattern in the next quarter.

She does it again,

and again.

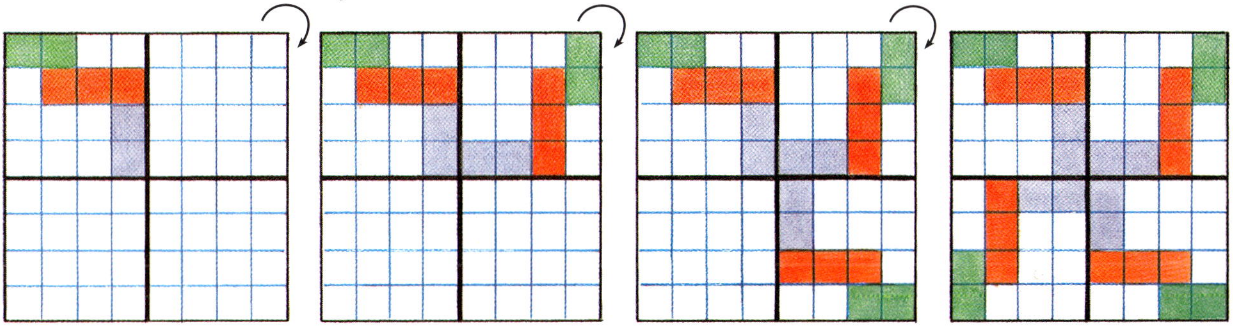

The finished pattern has order **4** rotational symmetry because in one rotation there are **4** positions in which the pattern looks the same.

Use squared paper to make your own pattern with order 4 rotational symmetry.

Unit 3 Weight

Writing weights

The total of this set of weights is:

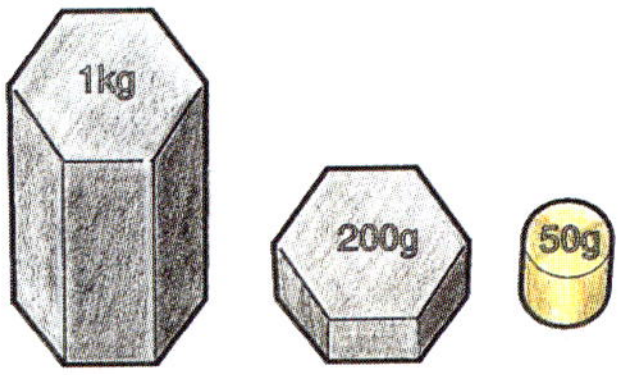

I kg + 200 g + 50 g or I kg 250 g or I250 g.

you need:
scales or balance and weights
objects to weigh

Show the total of each of these sets in three ways.

1
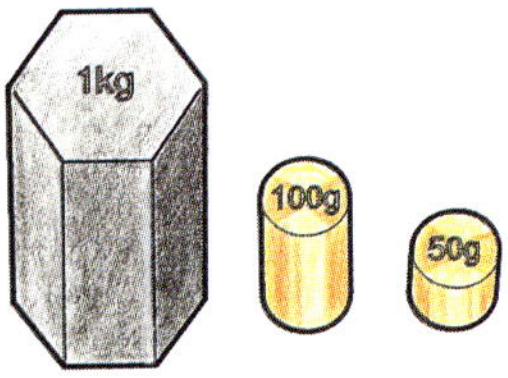

2
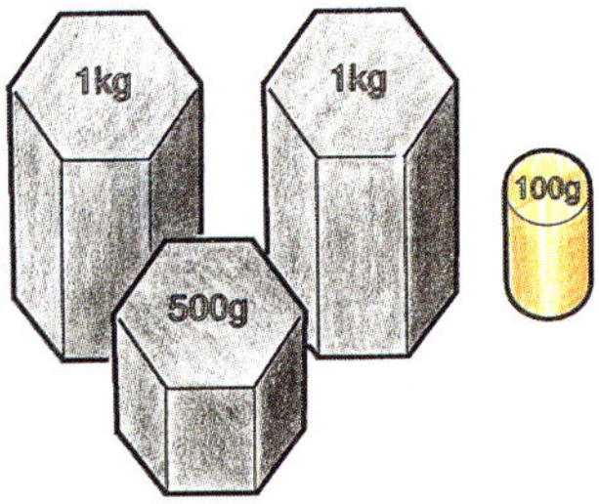

3
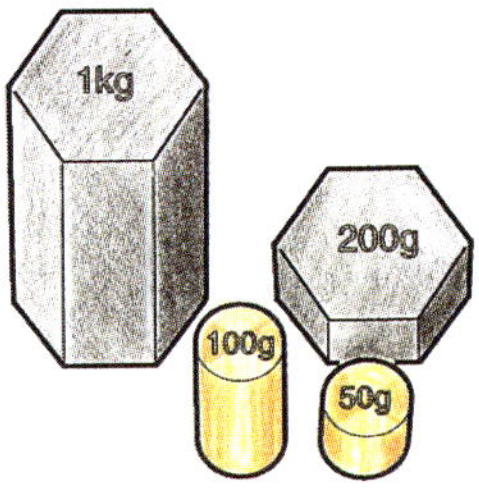

4
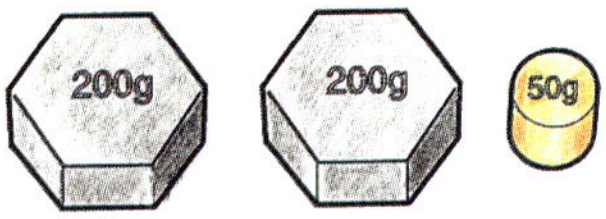

5
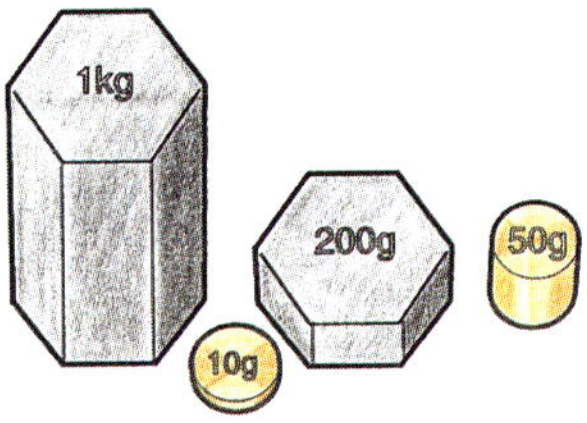

6
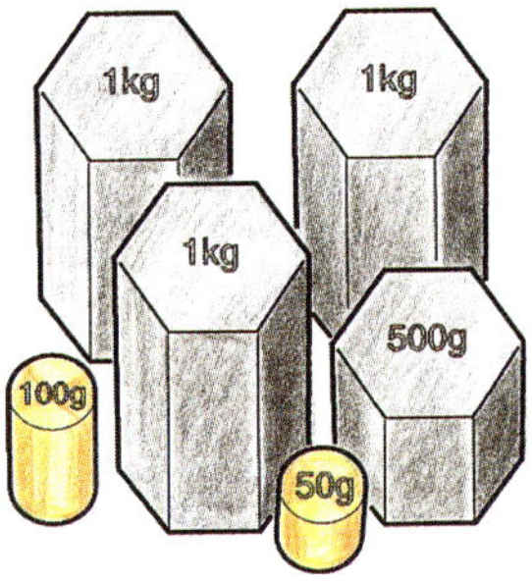

Write these weights as grams.

7 3 kg 750 g **8** I kg 300 g **9** 4 kg 255 g **10** 0 kg 500 g

Write these weights as kilograms and grams.

11 I246 g **12** 5400 g **13** 2655 g **14** I285 g

Find three objects that you think weigh more than I kg.

15 Weigh each object and record each weight as kilograms and grams and as grams.

16 Find the total weight of the three objects and record it in two ways.

Tonnes and tonnes

Remember: 1000 kg = 1 tonne

you need:
- calculator
- personal scales
- kitchen scales
- marbles
- Litre jug
- dry sand

1 Approximately how many children as heavy as you would weigh 1 tonne?

Twenty-five 1p coins weigh approximately 100 g.

2 Approximately how many 1p coins weigh 1 kg?

3 Approximately how many 1p coins weigh 1 tonne?

4 What is the value of 1 tonne of 1p coins?

5 How many marbles of the same size weigh 100 g?

6 Calculate how many marbles weigh 1 kg.

7 Calculate how many marbles weigh 1 tonne.

8 How much does a litre of dry sand weigh to the nearest kilogram?

9 Calculate approximately how many litres of sand weigh 1 tonne.

10 Do you think 1 tonne of sand would fill your classroom?

Unit 4 Handling Data 1

The school fun day

1 What is the lowest score?

2 What is the highest score?

3 Calculate the **range** of scores.

4 How many scores are there?

5 What is the total of all the scores?

6 Calculate the **mean** score.

Scores for the Ball in the bucket game

9 8 12 10 2 15 3 1 12

Find the **range** and **mean** of these scores.

7 **Darts scores**

17 38 14 15 26 10

8 **Skittles scores**

3 5 8 10 7 2 4 9 2 0

9 **Roll-a-ball scores**

25 10 25 30 15

10 **Hoop-la scores**

3 13 6 4 16 7 13 10

Write these scores in order.

Find the **median** (middle) and **mode** (most frequent) scores.

11 Scores so far

1 20 14 20 20 20 20 6 32 19 16

12 Scores so far

26 19 120 111 26 56 100 35 12

Letter count

Winston made this graph to show the numbers of letters in the names of the children in his class.

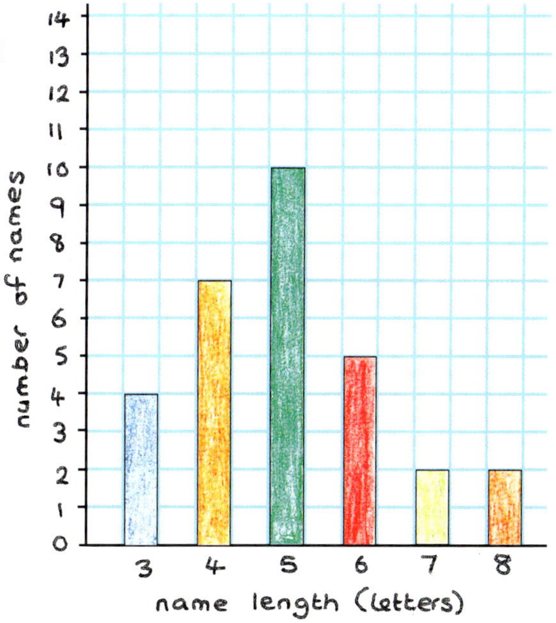

How many letters are there in:

1 the longest name?

2 the shortest name?

3 Calculate the **range** of name lengths.

4 What is the **mode** (most frequent) name length?

To find the total number of letters in all the names, Winston made a chart.

	number of letters
3 letters in 4 names	3×4 = 12
4 letters in 7 names	4×7 = 28
5 letters in 10 names	
6 letters in	
7 letters in	
8 letters in	
	Total

5 Copy and complete the chart.

6 How many names were surveyed?

7 What is the total number of letters?

8 Calculate the **mean** number of letters per name.

9 Can you think of a way of finding the **median** (middle) name length? Show how.

Unit 5 Angles

What's the angle?

you need:
protractor
ruler

Measure the angles. Copy the angles. Write the angle size in each one.

1

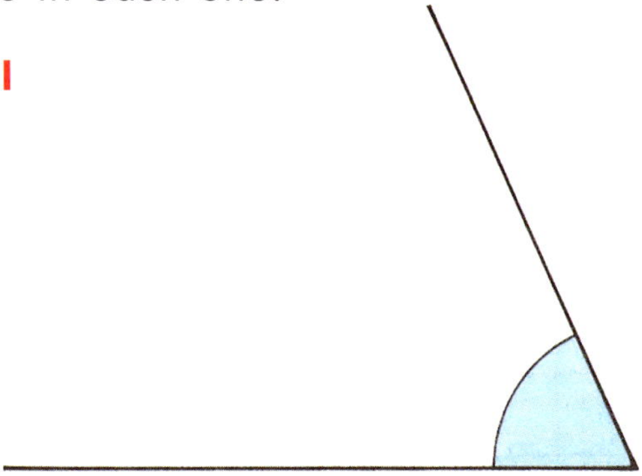

2

3

4

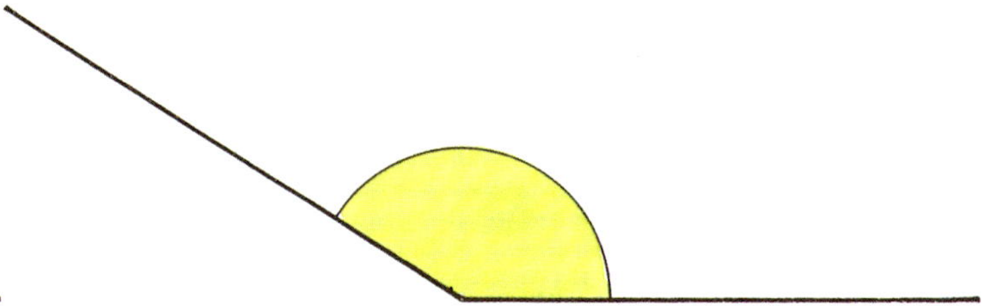

Measure the angles in each shape. Write the letter and the size of the angle.

5

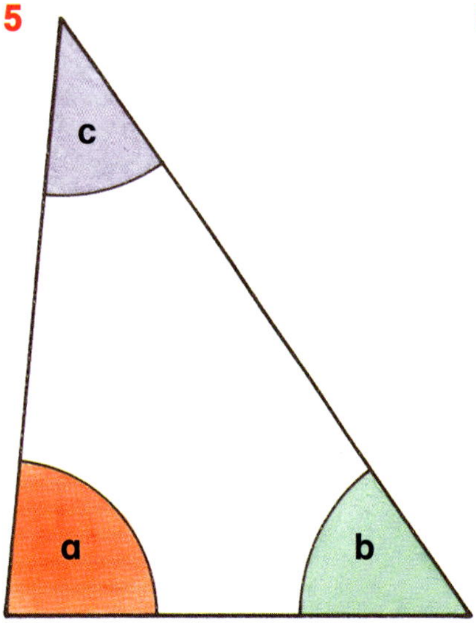

6

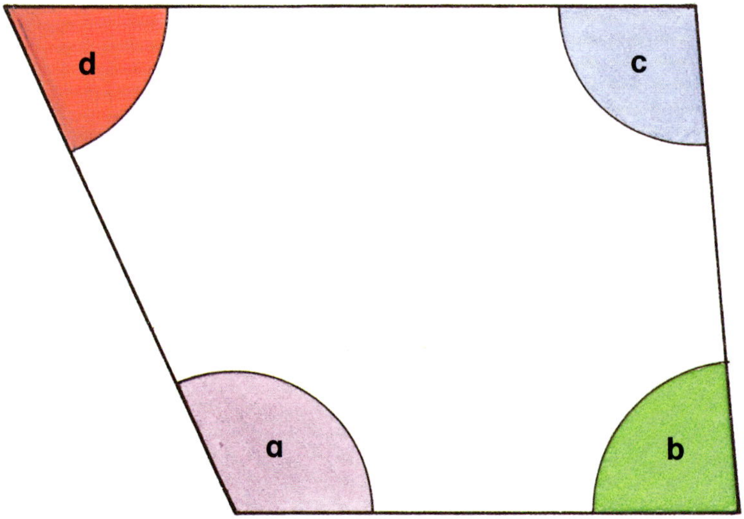

Angles in a triangle

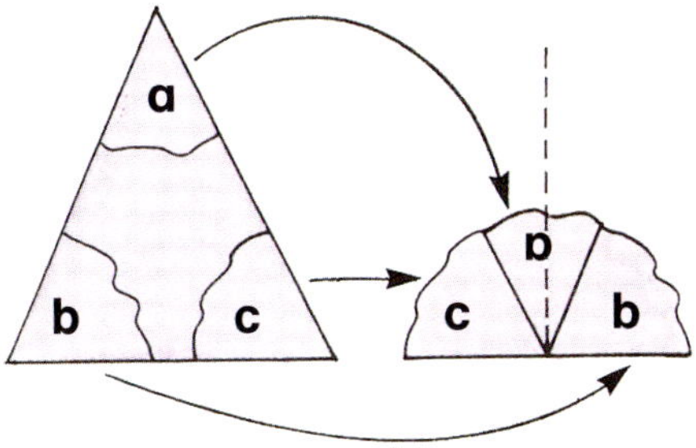

you need:

protractor

ruler

Remember, all the angles of a triangle together make two right angles (180°).

Draw a chart like this:
Measure the angles in each triangle below and record them in the chart.
Add the angles together and write the total for each triangle.

	angle			total
triangle	a	b	c	a + b + c
1				
2				
3				
4				

1

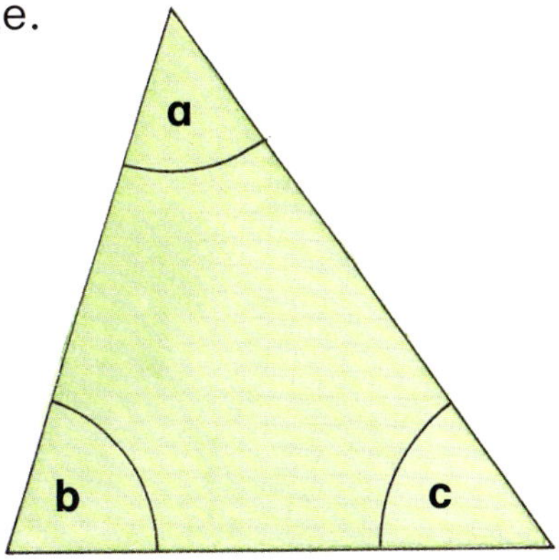

2

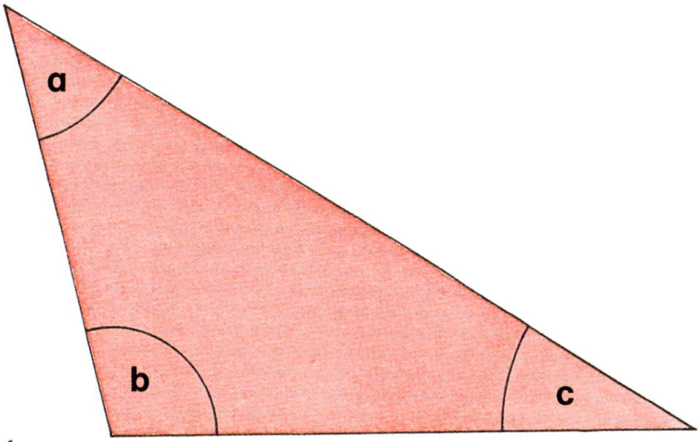

3

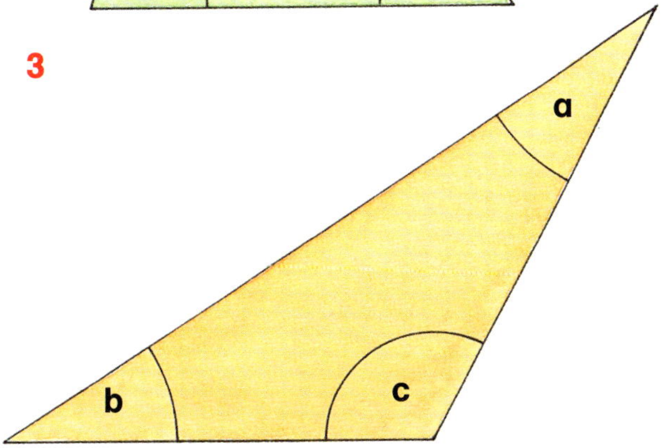

4

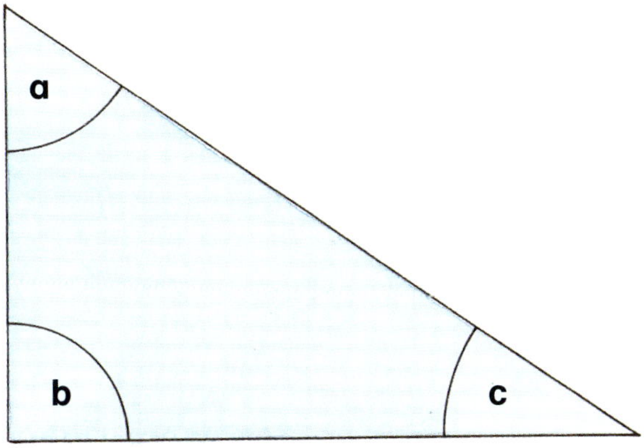

5 Draw two more triangles and record their data in the chart.

6 Are all the totals approximately 180°?

7 Are all the totals exactly 180°? If not, explain why.

Unit 6 Capacity and Volume

Capacity conversions

This amount can be shown in three ways:

1450 ml
1 l 450 ml
1·450 l

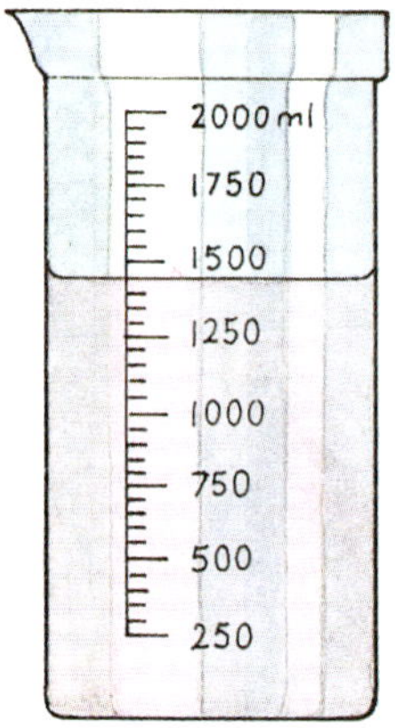

you need:
measuring cylinder
water
containers

Write each of these amounts in two more ways.

1 1550 ml
2 2250 ml
3 3400 ml
4 1 l 355 ml
5 2 l 475 ml
6 3 l 500 ml
7 1·800 l
8 1·000 l
9 2·075 l

Make a collection of containers that you think will hold more than a litre altogether.

Use water and a measuring cylinder to find out how much they hold altogether.

10 Do they hold more than a litre altogether?

11 Record the total amount in three ways.

12 Repeat the activity with another collection of containers.

By how many millilitres has the level of the water risen?

13

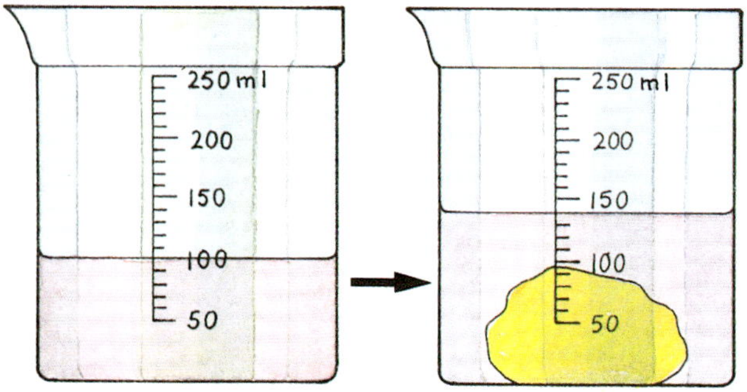

14

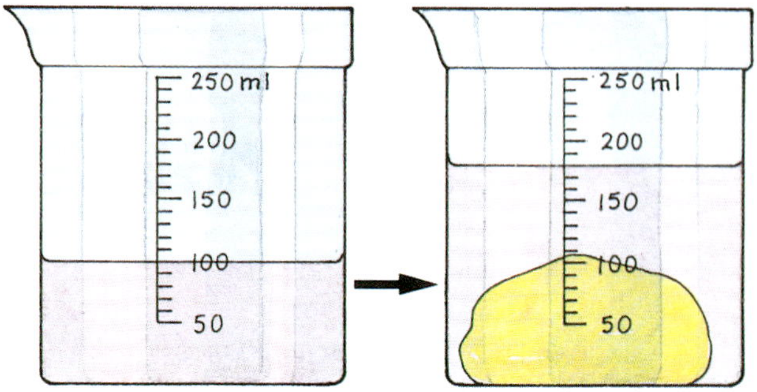

you need:

- 1 cm squared paper or card
- scissors, glue
- measuring cylinder
- centimetre cubes
- sand, spoon

Different boxes can hold the same amounts

1 Draw this net of an open cuboid box on 1 cm squared paper or card.

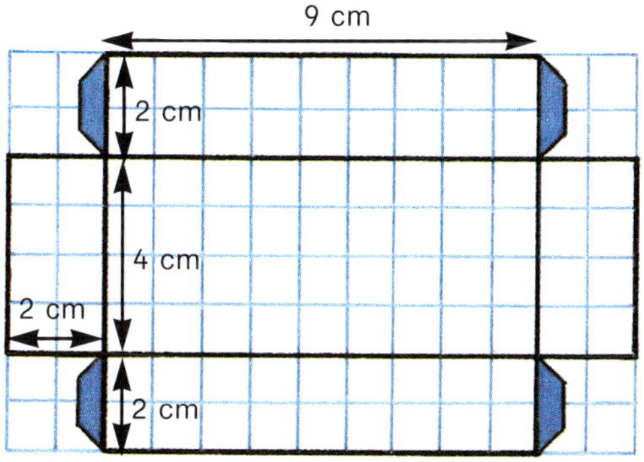

2 Make the box.

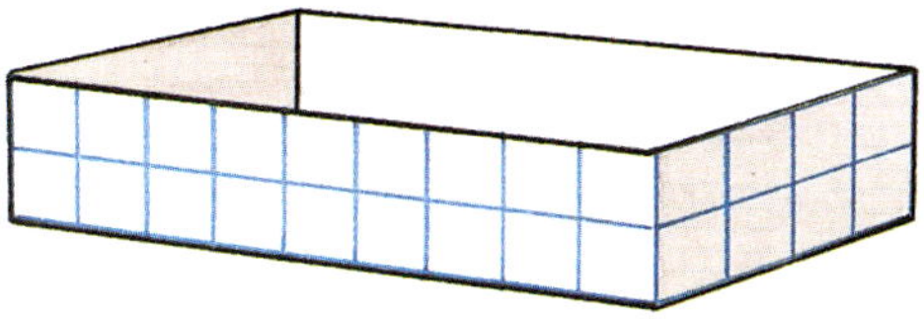

3 Use centimetre cubes to find the volume of the box.

4 How many millilitres of sand will the box hold?

5 Check using sand and a measuring cylinder.

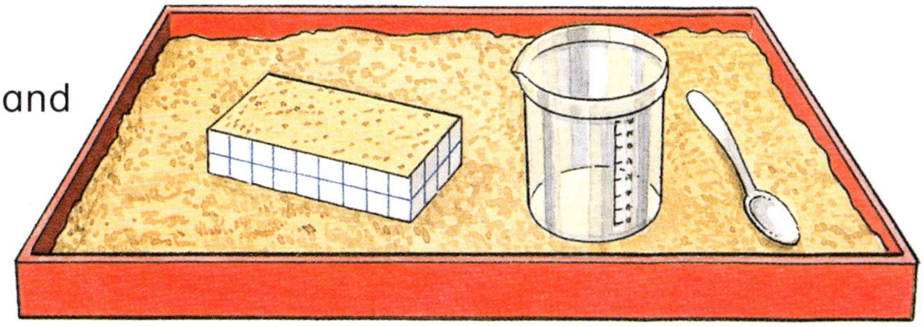

6 Make a different box that will hold the same amount of sand.

7 Record the length, height and width of the box.

8 Make a box that will hold half the amount of each of the above boxes.

9 Record the length, height and width of the box.

10 Make an open cube that will hold 27 ml of sand.

11 Record the length of the sides of the cube.

Unit 7 Quadrilaterals 1

Shape Search

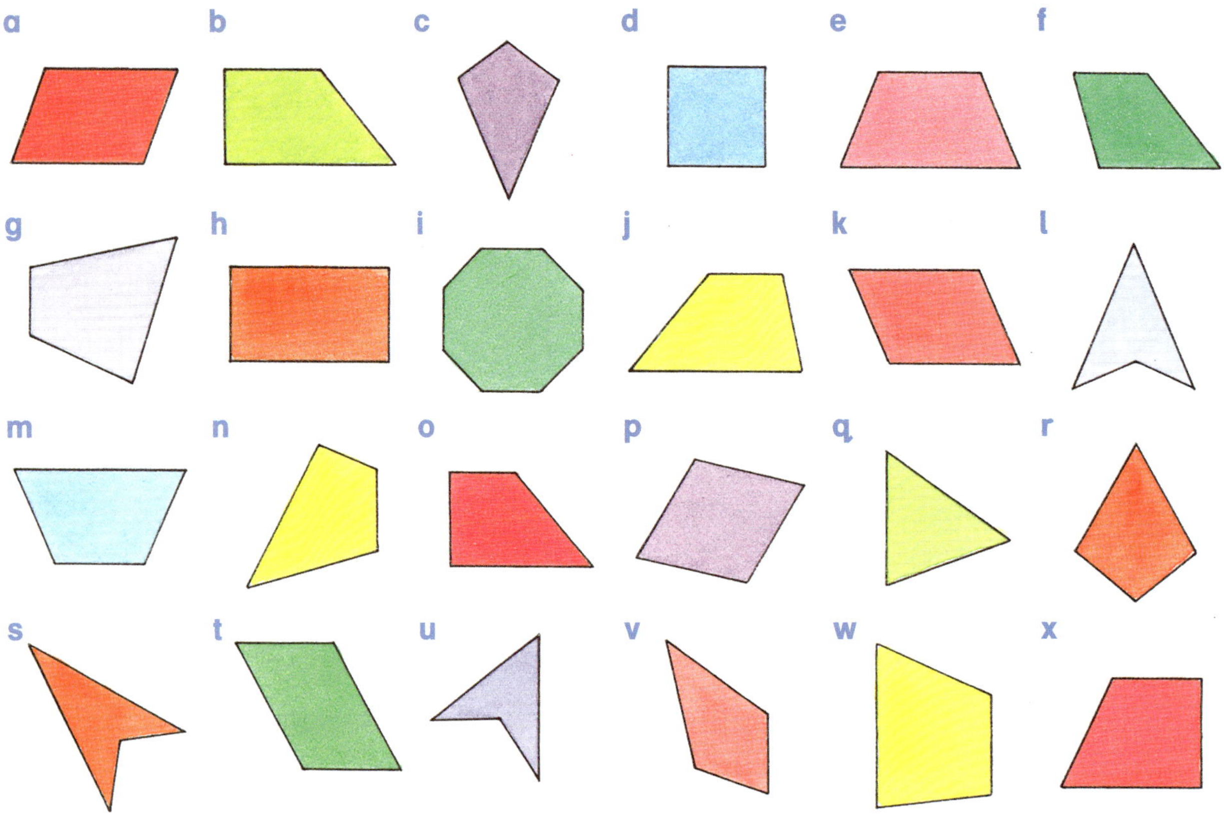

1 Which shapes are **not** quadrilaterals?

Which quadrilaterals are:

2 kites?

3 arrowheads?

4 Which quadrilaterals have parallel sides?

Which quadrilaterals are:

5 parallelograms?

6 trapeziums?

Which trapeziums are:

7 right-angled?

8 isosceles?

you need:
plain paper
scissors
5 mm or 1 cm squared or square dotty paper

Paper folding

1 Follow these instructions to make an isosceles triangle by folding and cutting a sheet of paper.

Fold one side in half to find the mid-point.

Make folds from the mid-point to the opposite corners.

Cut along the folds.

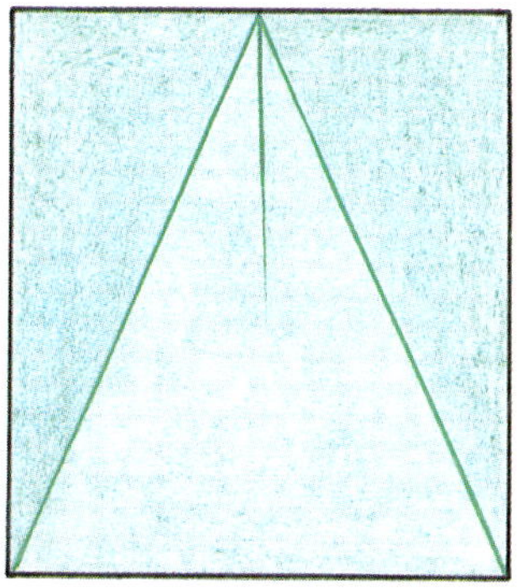

2 Fold and cut the triangle to make an isosceles trapezium.

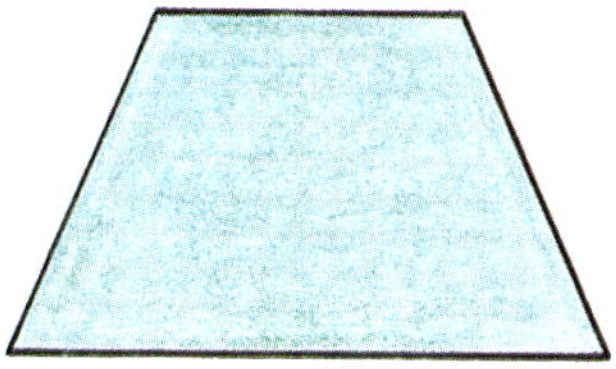

Just by folding a sheet of paper and cutting along folds, make:

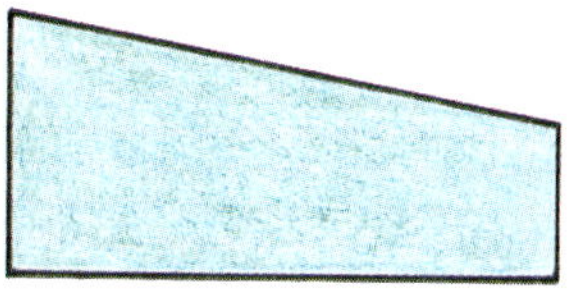

3 a right-angled trapezium

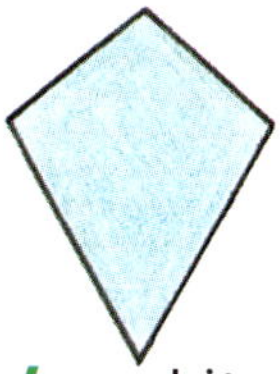

4 a kite

5 an arrowhead

Arrowhead investigation

Start with an arrowhead like this on squared or square dotty paper.

Keep the two longer sides fixed.

Investigate what happens as you move the vertex down step by step.

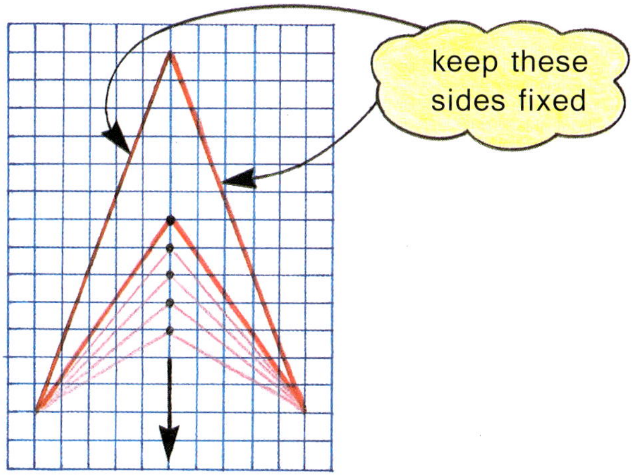

6 What happens to the angles?

7 What shapes does the arrowhead gradually turn into?

Unit 8 Probability

What chance?

0 — less than (<) $\frac{1}{2}$ — $\frac{1}{2}$ — more than (>) $\frac{1}{2}$ — 1

impossible — poor chance — **even chance** — good chance — **certain**

Write **impossible**, **poor chance**, **even chance**, **good chance** or **certain** for how likely these events are.

1 You will sleep at school tonight.

2 When a dice is thrown, the result is a six.

3 You will watch television tonight.

4 It will snow tomorrow.

5 When you draw from a normal pack of playing cards, the result is a green card.

Write 0, $<\frac{1}{2}$, $\frac{1}{2}$, $>\frac{1}{2}$ or 1 to show the chance of the arrow landing on:

6 red 7 blue 8 green

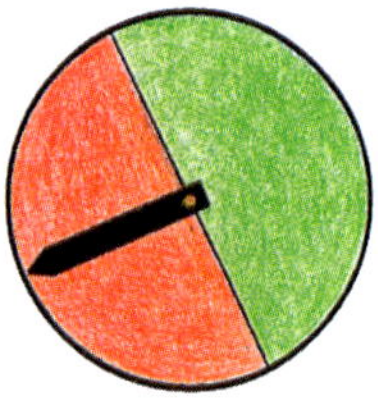

9 green 10 blue 11 yellow

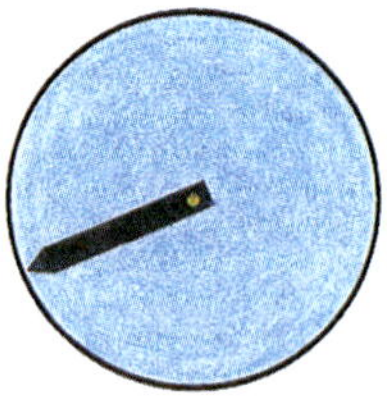

12 red 13 green 14 yellow

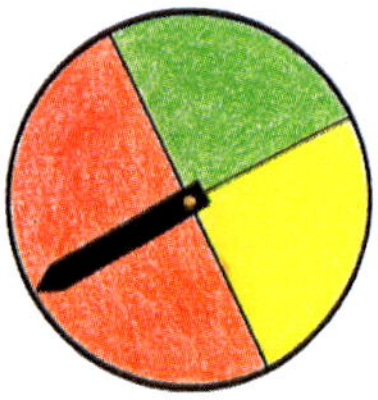

15 green 16 red 17 blue

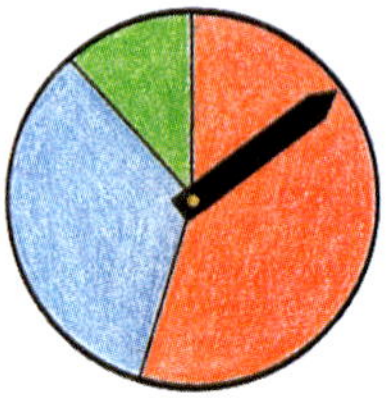

Dicey business

you need:

- 1 cm squared paper
- two dice

A game is played by throwing two dice and adding the two numbers to get a score.

first dice

second dice

+	1	2	3	4	5	6
1	2					
2			5			
3					8	
4				8		
5		7				
6			9			12

1 Copy and complete this grid to show all the possible combinations of dice numbers and the scores.

2 Make a frequency table to show the frequency of all scores in the grid.

3 What are the two least likely scores?

4 What is the most likely score?

5 What scores less than 15 are impossible?

score	frequency
2	
3	
4	
5	
6	

Throw a pair of dice 50 times.

6 Make a tally chart, then a graph, to show the frequency of each score.

7 Are the results what you expected?

8 Write about your results.

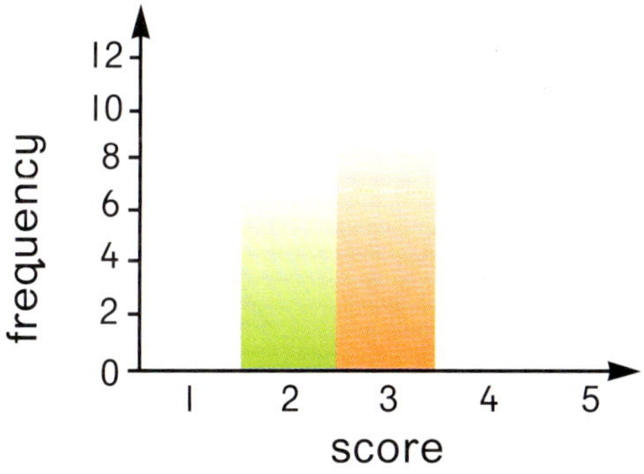

Ask your teacher if you can make a display about this activity to show other children what you did and what you found out.

Unit 9 2-D Shape

you need:
protractor
compasses
ruler

Shapes from plans

Draw shapes using the information on these plans.

1

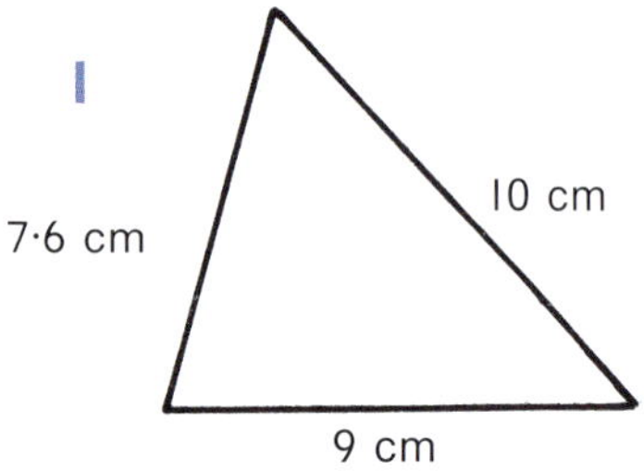

2

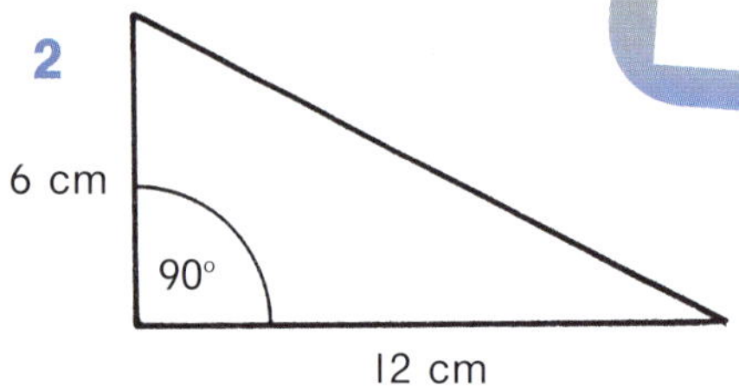

3

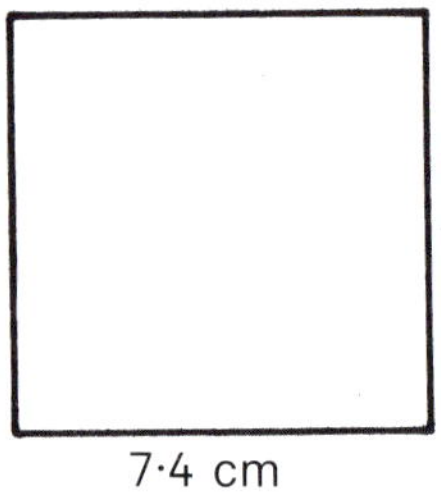

square

4

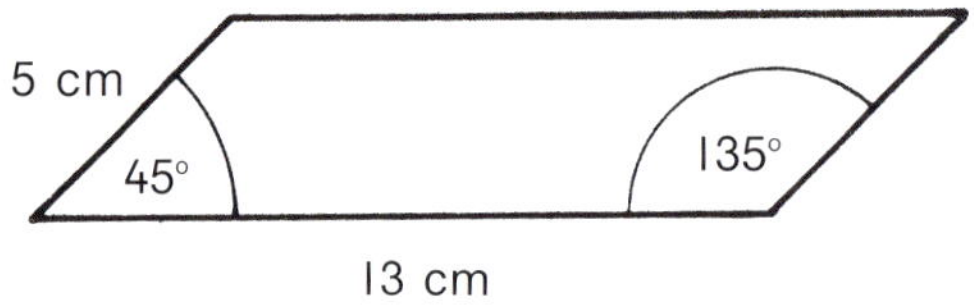

parallelogram

Odd man out

Which pair of shapes in each row are congruent to each other?

5

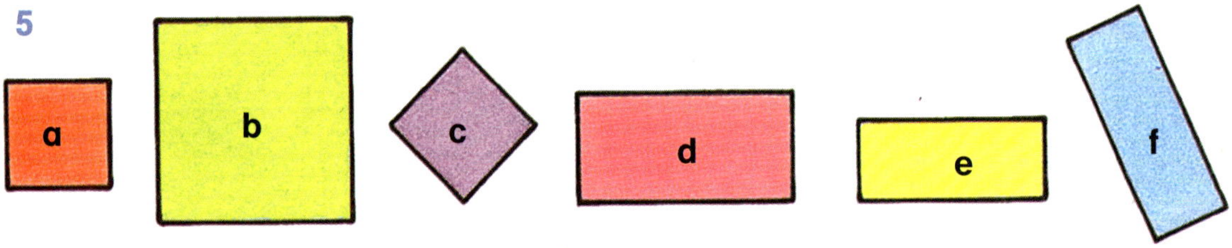

6

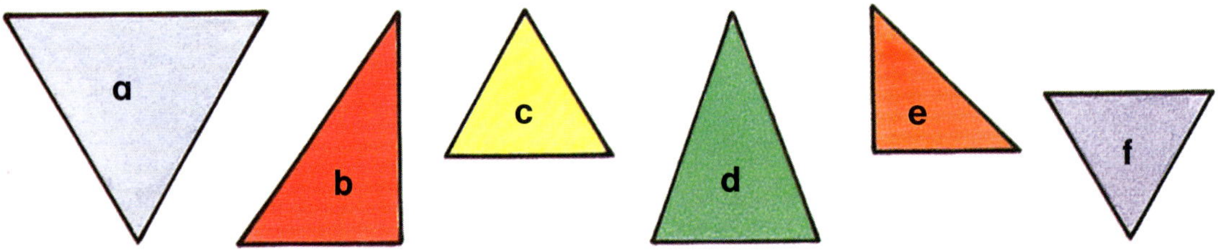

7

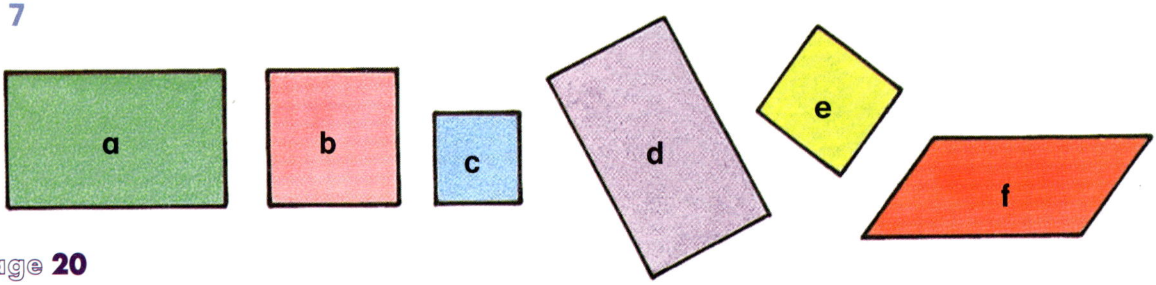

you need:

compasses

ruler

protractor

Copycat

Copy these designs as accurately as you can.
In each design, look for shapes that are congruent to each other and colour them the same.

1

Hint: draw the square first.

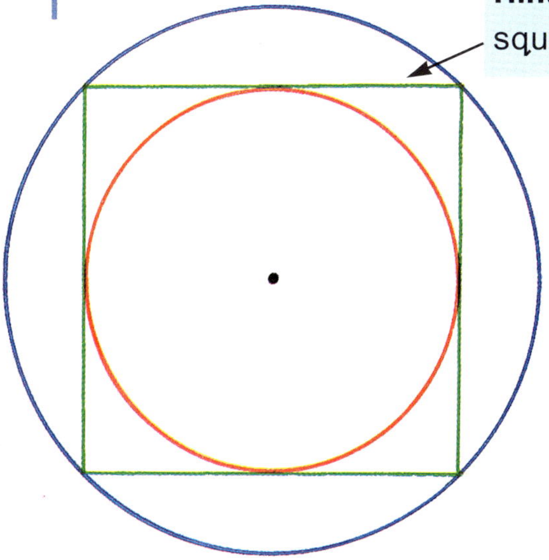

2

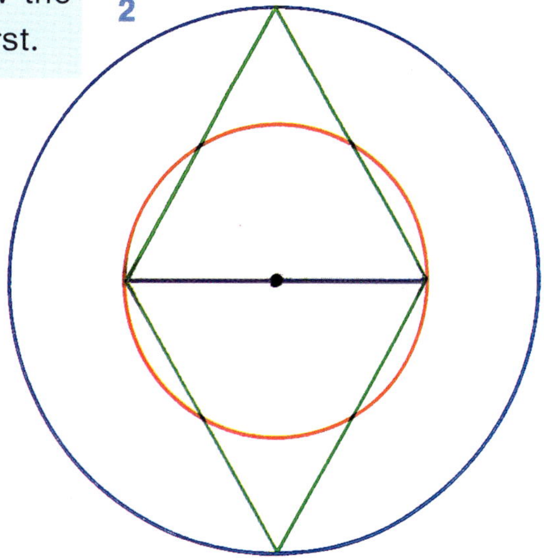

These lines are the diagonals of quadrilaterals. Predict what sort of quadrilateral the diagonals belong to. Measure the diagonals and the angles between them. Draw the diagonals and complete the shapes.

3

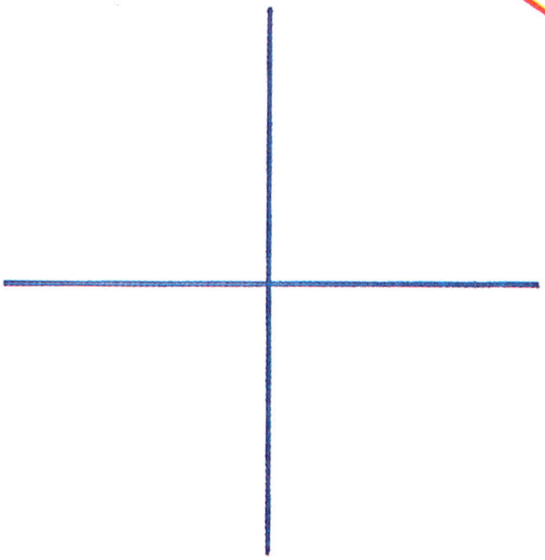

4

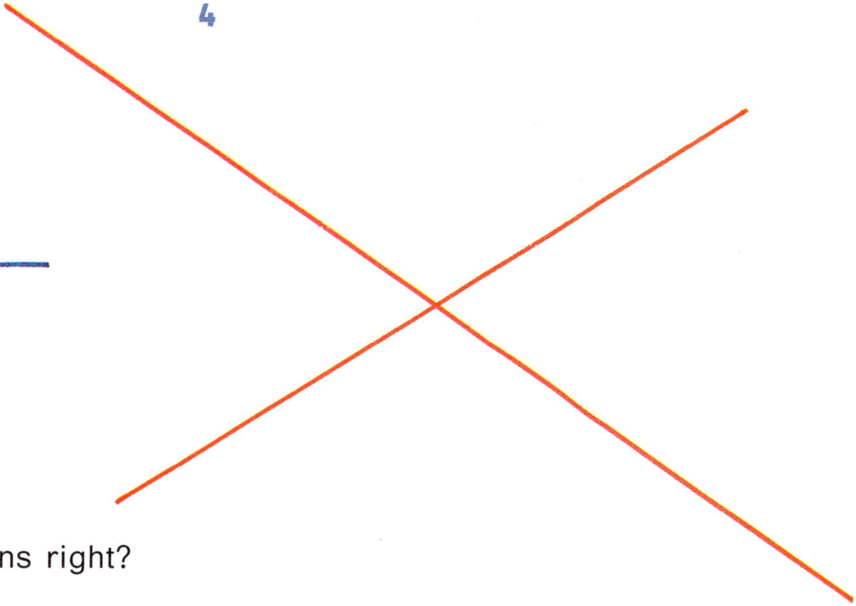

5 Were your predictions right?

Unit 10 Volume

Dimensions dilemmas

you need:
centimetre cubes
calculator

Calculate the volume of each cuboid in cubic centimetres.

1

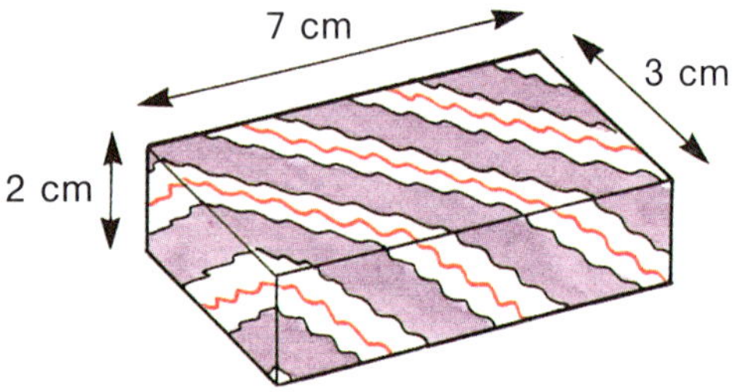

2

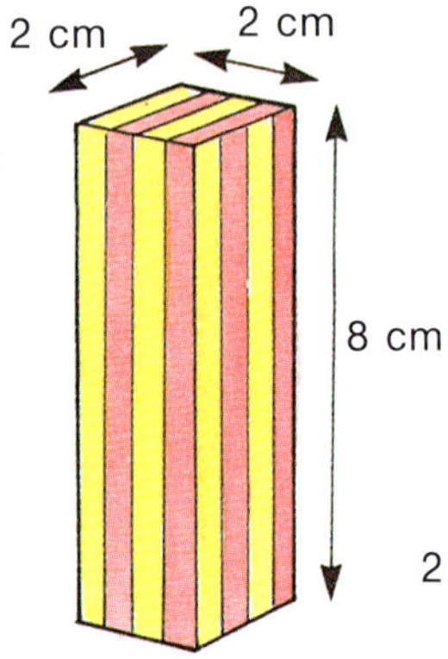

3

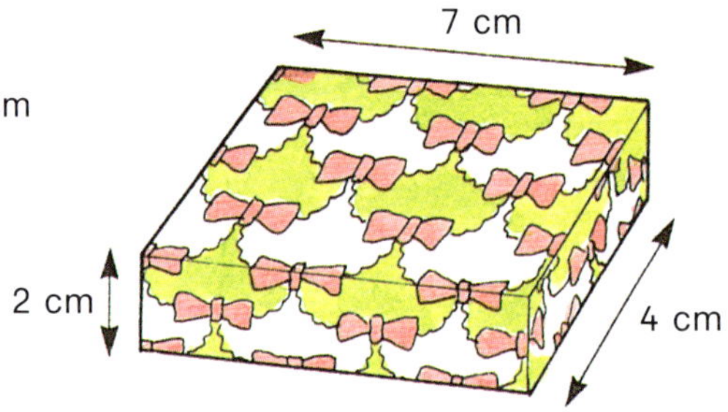

Check that your answers are correct by making the cuboids using centimetre cubes.

Work out the missing dimensions for these cuboids.

4

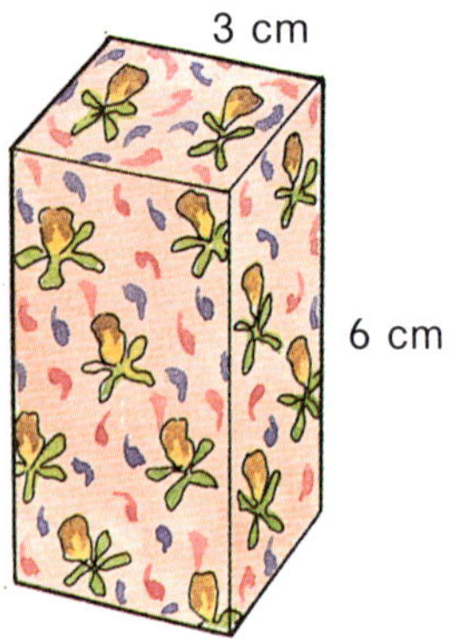

volume = 36 cm^3

5

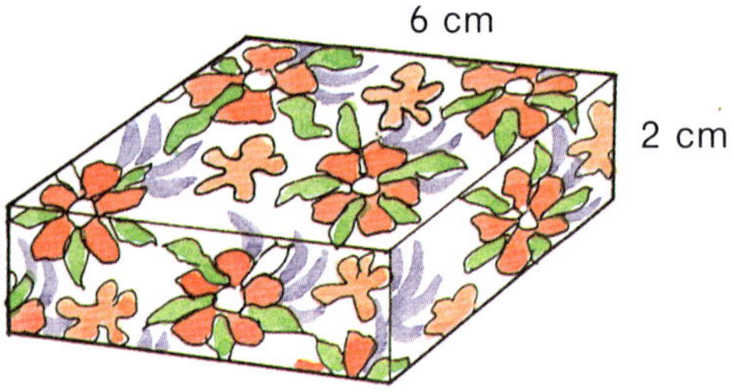

volume = 60 cm^3

6

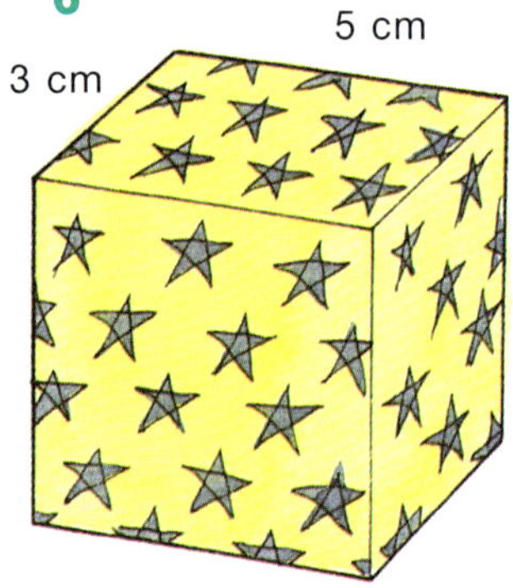

volume = 75 cm^3

Check your answers by making the cuboids.

7 Describe the dimensions of three cuboids that will each have a volume of 48 cm^3.

Twice as big!

you need:
Multilink cubes

Wizard Well-to-do put a spell on his treasure chest to make it twice as big, but he forgot about the key.

This is the shape and size of the key.

Can you make it twice as big so that it will fit the treasure chest?

Think about what 'twice as big' means.

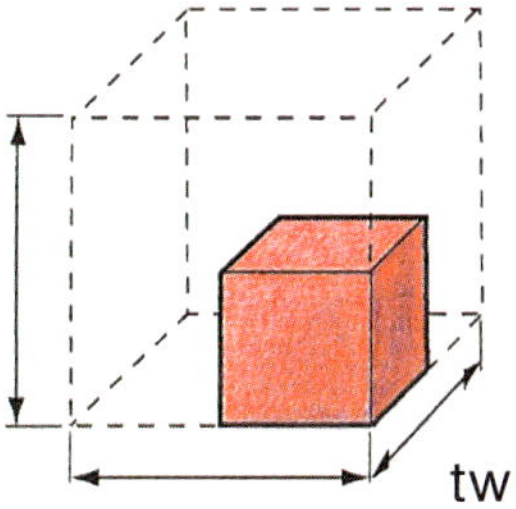

Copy and complete these sentences.

1 The volume of the small key is ☐ cubes.

2 The volume of the large key is ☐ cubes.

3 To make the key twice as big I need ☐ times as many cubes.

Look at your answer for **3**.

4 Can you explain why?

Unit 11 Transformations

Moving shapes

you need:
5 mm or 1 cm squared paper
mirror

Draw a co-ordinates grid like this.

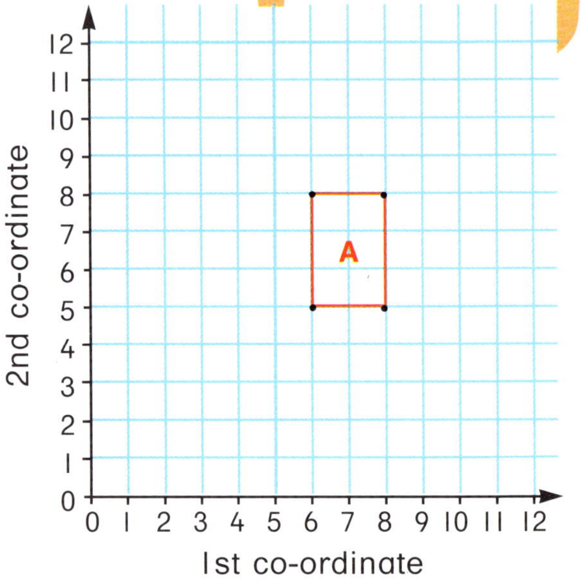

1 Mark these co-ordinate points and join them, in order, to make shape A.

(6, 8) (8, 8) (8, 5) (6, 5)

2 Follow the instructions in the box below to change the co-ordinates. Draw the new shape each time.

Each time write the letter of the new shape and say how many squares, to the left, to the right, up or down, shape A moved to make the new shape.

Starting co-ordinates: (6, 8) (8, 8) (8, 5) (6, 5)

new shape	instruction
B	Add 4 to the first co-ordinate in each pair.
C	Subtract 5 from the first co-ordinate in each pair.
D	Add 3 to the second co-ordinate in each pair.
E	Subtract 4 from the second co-ordinate in each pair.

Copy each shape and mirror line onto squared paper. Draw and colour the reflection. Use a mirror to check.

3

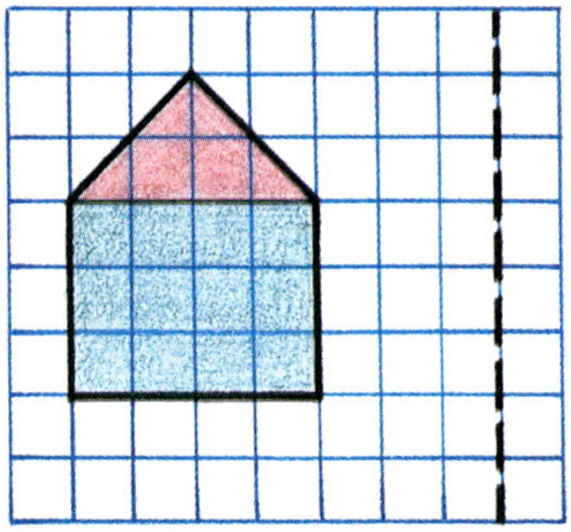

4

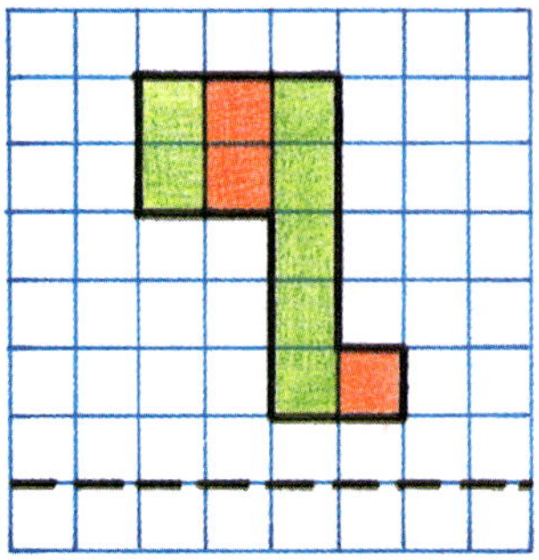

5

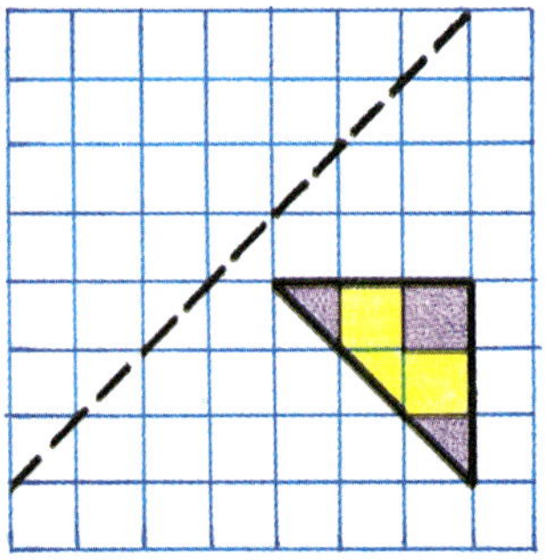

you need:

5 mm or 1 cm squared paper

Investigating slides

Draw a co-ordinates grid like this.

Mark these points and join them in order to make starting shape A.

(5, 10) (7, 10) (7, 8) (5, 8)

Investigate what happens when you:

1 Add 4 to **both** co-ordinates in each pair to make a new shape B.

2 Subtract 4 from **both** co-ordinates in each pair to make a new shape C.

Each time describe the movement from the starting shape to the new shape.

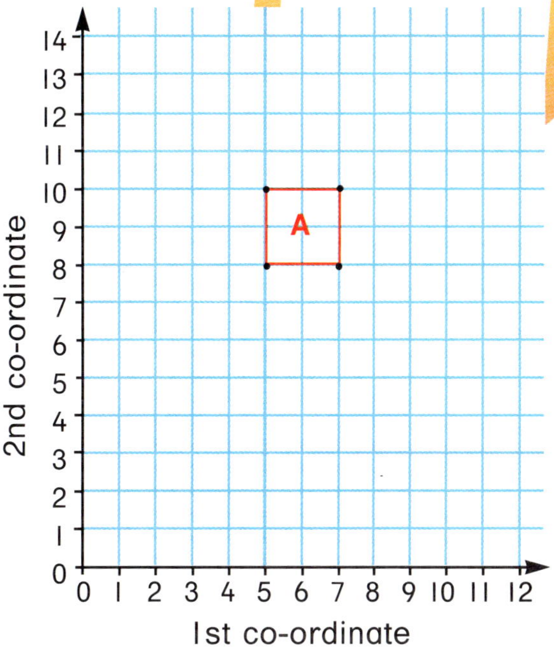

On the grid below, what has been done to the co-ordinates of shape A to make shape B each time?

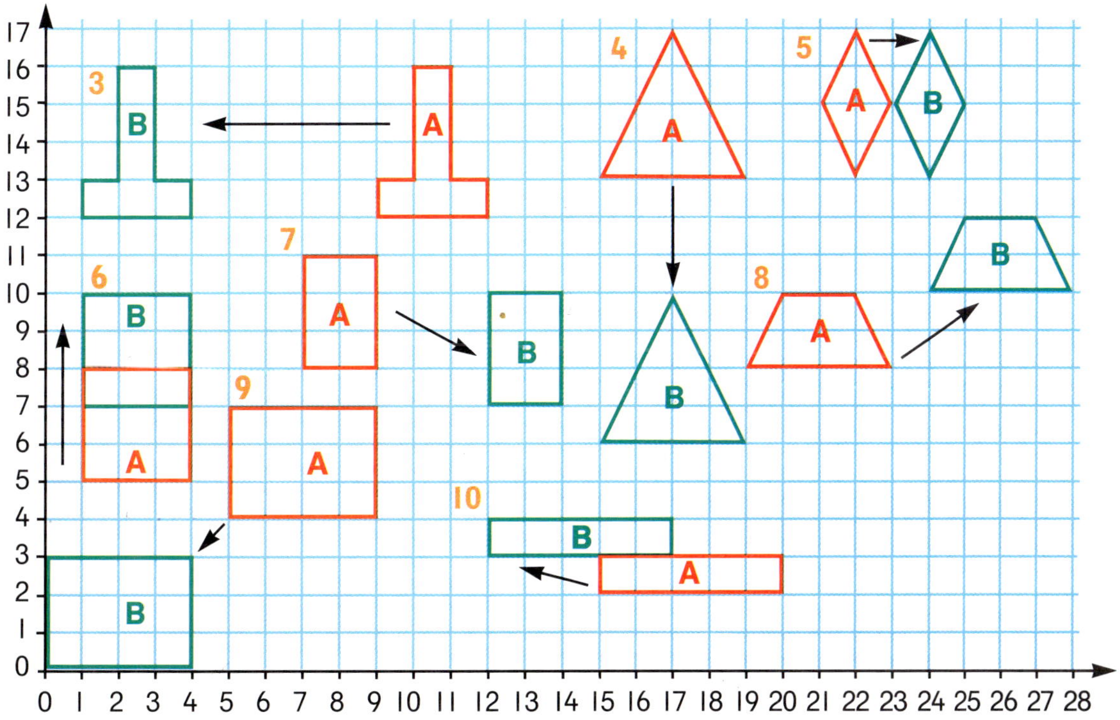

Unit 12 Time

Times of day

you need:
squared paper

Here is a plan of Danny's day.

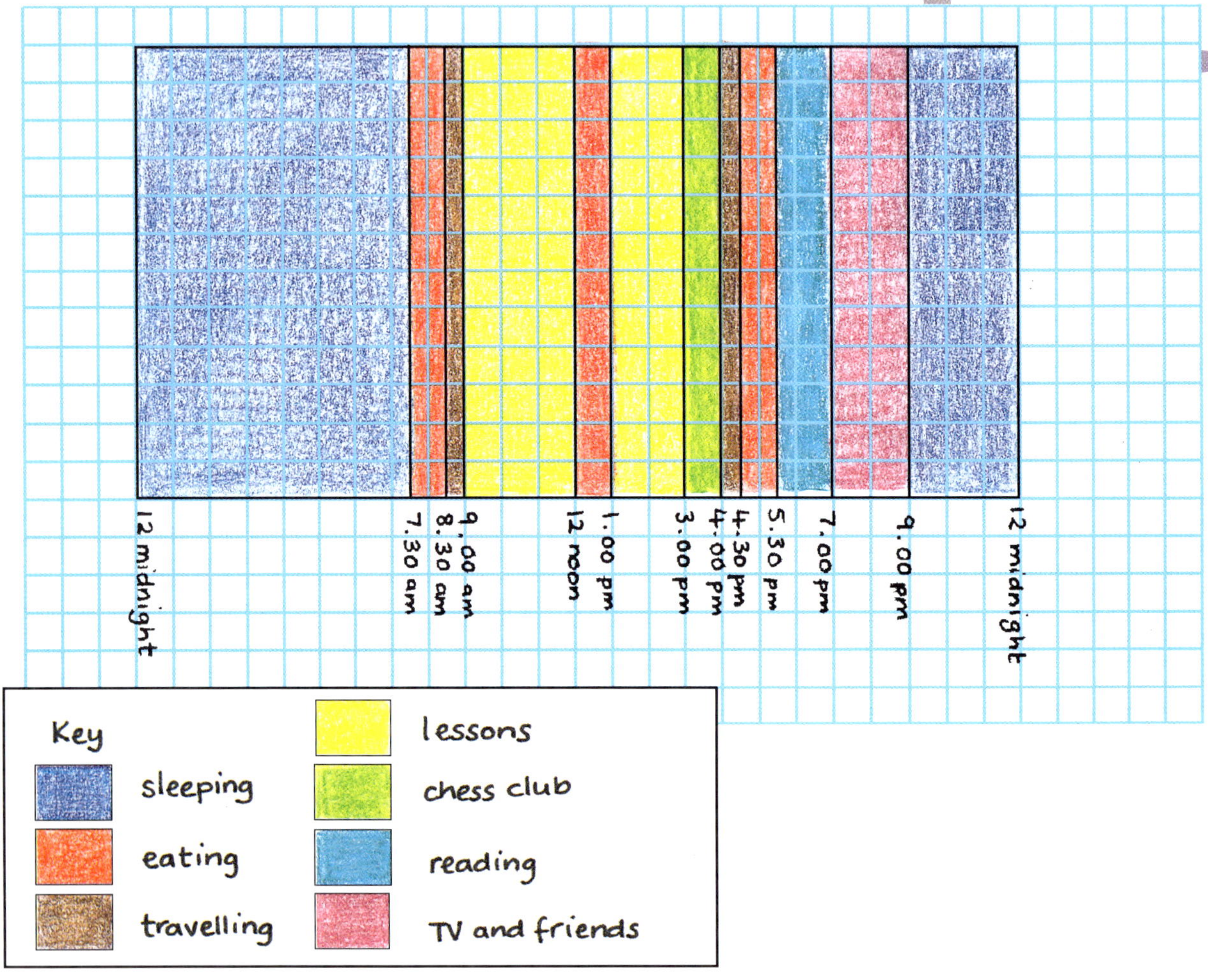

1 What time does school finish?

2 What time does Danny arrive home?

3 What length of time is Danny in bed?

4 How long does he take to get to school?

5 Make a plan of a day in your life.

Write three questions you could answer with your plan.

TV times

TV VIEWING

TUESDAY 10TH

BBC 1	BBC 2	ITV	CHANNEL 4
3.35 Blinky Bill	2.10 Conference Live	3.50 Hot Rod Dogs	4.30 Fifteen to One
4.00 Oscar's Orchestra	5.30 Floyd on Italy	4.05 The Twisted Tales of Felix the Cat	5.00 The Oprah Winfrey Show
4.25 Animal Hospital	6.00 Fresh Prince of Bel Air	4.15 Hurricanes	5.50 Murun Buchstans-angur
5.00 Newsround	6.25 Heartbreak High	4.40 The Ward	6.00 The Avengers
5.10 Byker Grove	7.10 Dear Dilemma	5.10 After 5	7.00 News
5.35 Neighbours		5.40 News and Weather	
6.00 News		5.55 Your Shout	
6.30 Regional News		6.00 Home and Away	
7.00 Island Race		6.30 London Tonight	
		7.00 Emmerdale	

1 If you could choose what you were going to watch, but no more than one hour of television, which programmes would you watch?

2 What would the total time be?

Remember to use 24-hour clock times to set the video. Which starting and finishing times would you set to record:

3 Home and Away?   4 Byker Grove?   5 Heartbreak High?

Keep a careful record of all the times you watch television for a week.

6 On which day do you watch most television?

7 How many hours do you watch in total for the week?

Unit 13 Quadrilaterals 2

Making and drawing quadrilaterals

you need:

geo-strips and paper fasteners or straws and pipe cleaners

square dotty paper

ruler

Use paper fasteners and 2 different lengths of geo-strip

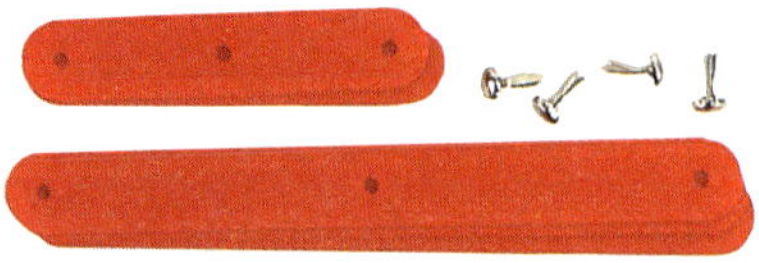

or pipe cleaners and 2 different lengths of straw.

Make these shapes. Write the name of each shape you have made.

1

2

3

4

5

6

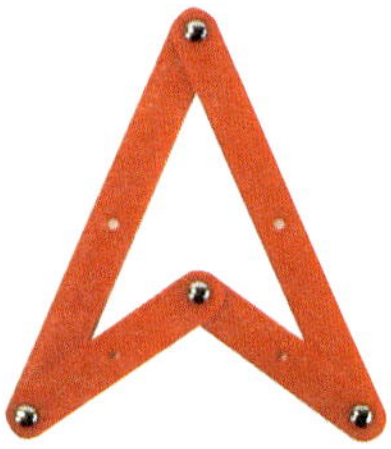

Each of shapes 1 to 6, when pushed, will change into another shape that has the same length edges but different angles.

7 Write the names of each pair of shapes that will change from one to the other when pushed.

8 Use square dotty paper and a ruler to draw these shapes:

a kite	a rhombus
a trapezium	a rectangle
an arrowhead	a square
a parallelogram	

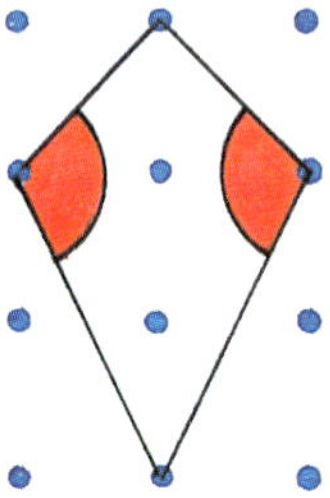

On each one, colour any angles that are the same.

Cut and slide tessellations

Start with a shape that has opposite edges equal in length.

Cut a shape from one edge. Slide it to the opposite edge and tape it in place.

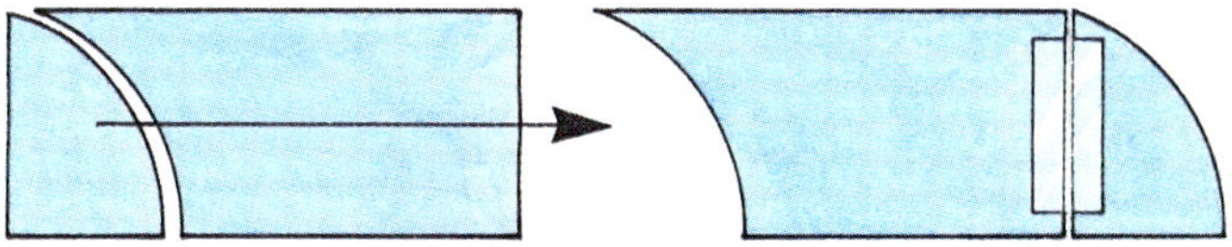

Draw round your new shape. Cut it out and use it to make a tessellating pattern.

Make your own cut and slide tessellation.

You can start with a rectangle, a parallelogram or a rhombus.

A challenge

A more complicated tessellation can be made by cutting and sliding on both equal edges.

Try it.

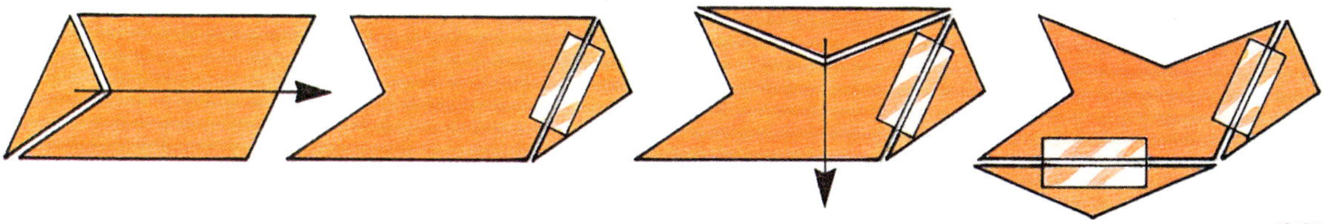

Unit 14 Decision Trees

Minibeast differences

you need:
large sheets of paper

worm

snail

honey-bee

spider

Write one difference between each of these pairs of minibeasts.

1 worm, snail

2 worm, spider

3 worm, honey-bee

4 snail, spider

5 snail, honey-bee

6 spider, honey-bee

Copy and complete these decision trees to sort each minibeast into a group of its own.

7

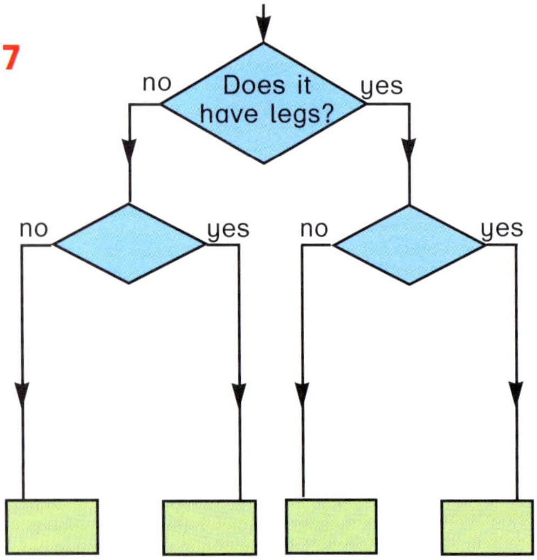

8

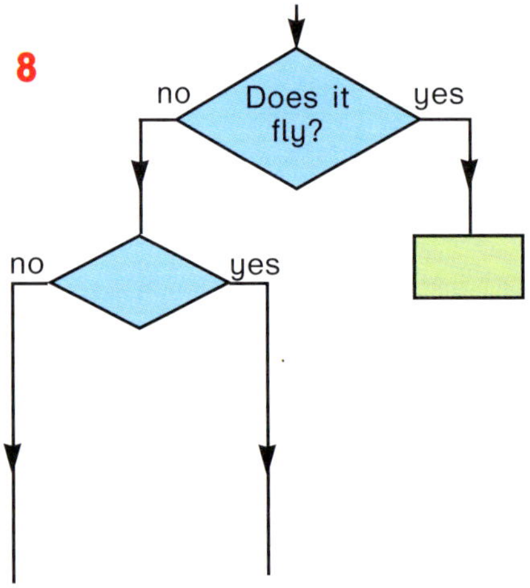

9 Make a decision tree to sort each of these animals into a group of its own.

robin

fieldmouse

butterfly

centipede

you need:
- pack of playing cards
- large sheet of paper

Card sort

1 On a large sheet of paper, make a decision tree that sorts each of the cards above into a group of its own.

2 Play this game with a friend.

Take the eight cards above from a pack of playing cards.

Shuffle them and spread them face down.

Your friend chooses one of the cards and looks at it.

You ask the questions on the decision tree one by one to work out which card was chosen.

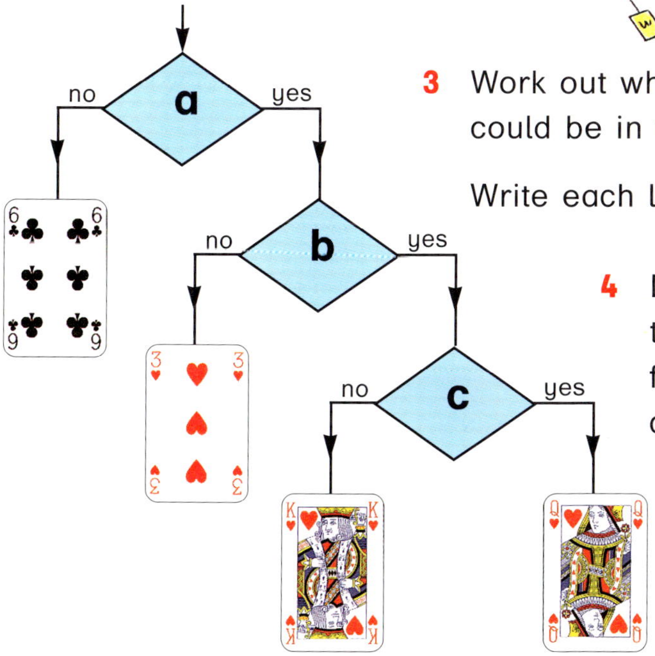

3 Work out what the questions could be in this decision tree.

Write each letter and the question.

4 Draw another decision tree to sort the cards where the first question sorts the four cards into two **equal** groups.

Unit 15 Area

you need:
1 cm squared paper
ruler

Areas

Measure the length and width of each small rectangle.
Find the area of each small rectangle.
Add them to find the area of the whole shape.

1

2

3

Find the area of the rectangle.
Then find the area of the triangle.

4

5

6

On centimetre squared paper, draw right-angled triangles with these areas.

7 16 cm^2 **8** 26 cm^2 **9** 36 cm^2

Hint: Draw rectangles first. What will the areas of the rectangles need to be?

you need:
ruler

Combining triangles and rectangles

Find the areas of these shapes. Show how you worked them out.

1
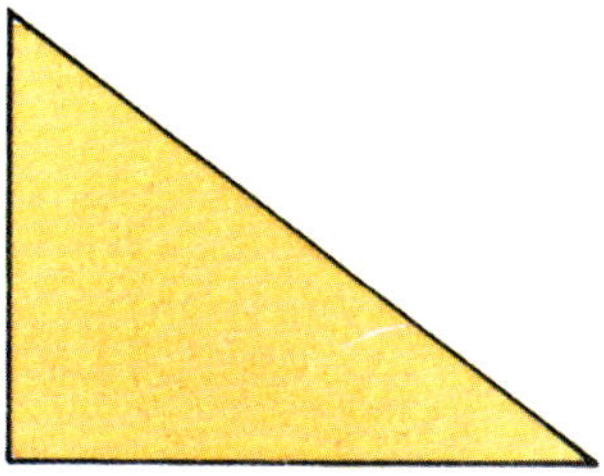

2
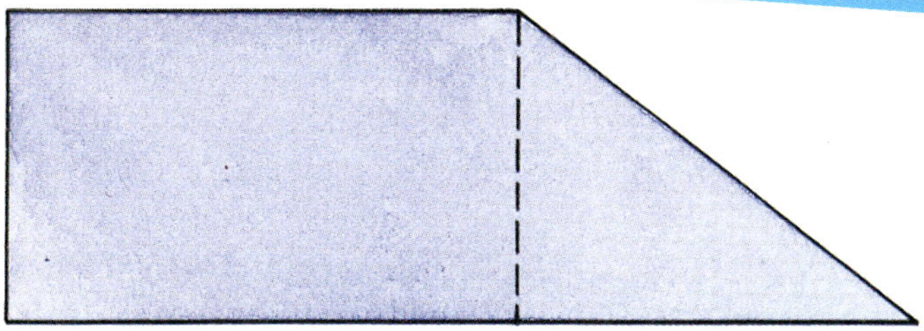

3
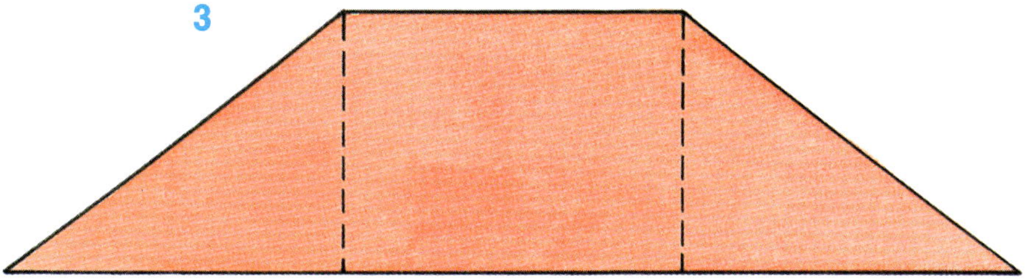

4
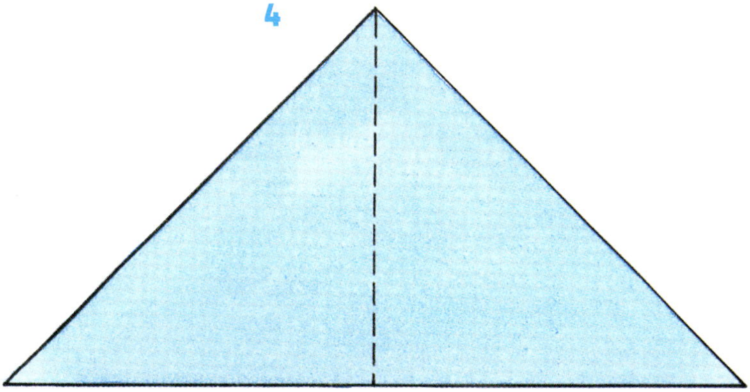

5
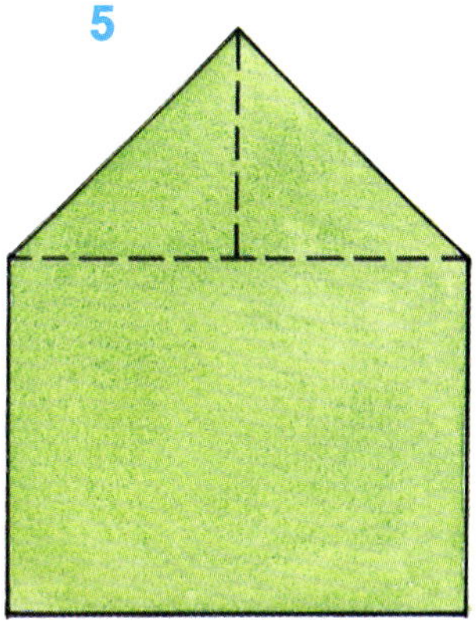

6

Unit 16 Handling Data 2

Traffic survey

This pie chart shows the types of vehicle that passed the school in one day.

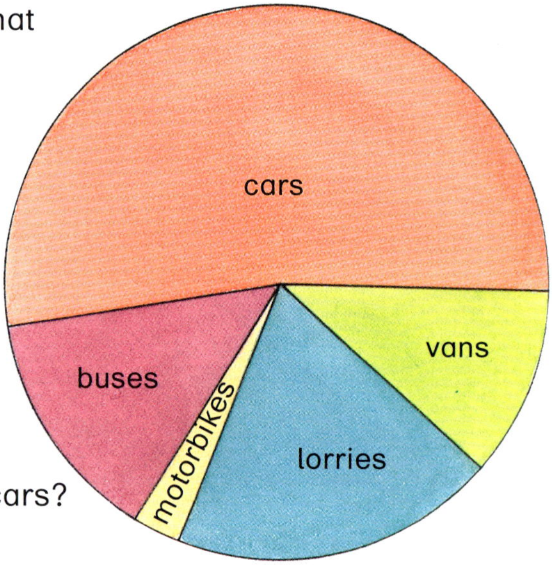

1 Of which type of vehicle were there most?

2 Of which type of vehicle were there fewest?

3 Were there more lorries than vans?

4 Were there more buses than lorries?

5 Were more than half of the vehicles cars?

6 Were there more vans than buses?

7 Were less than a quarter of the vehicles vans?

This pie chart shows the colour of 100 cars that passed the school in one day.

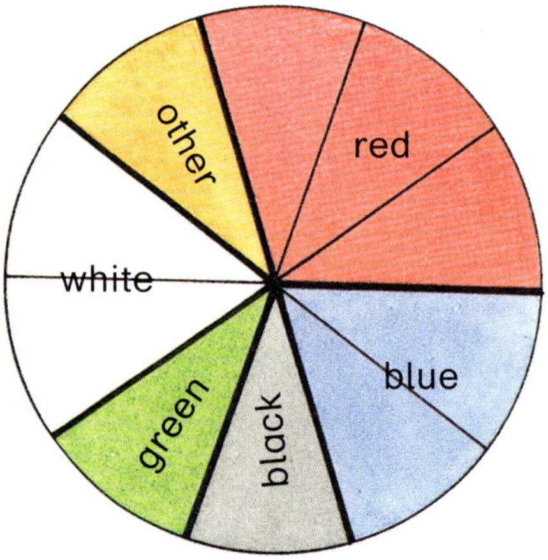

8 List the colours. By each colour, write the fraction of cars and the number of cars of that colour.

you need:
squared paper
ruler
compasses

Pie chart day

Frances worked out to the nearest hour how long she spent on different activities during one complete day.

She showed the results on this pie chart.

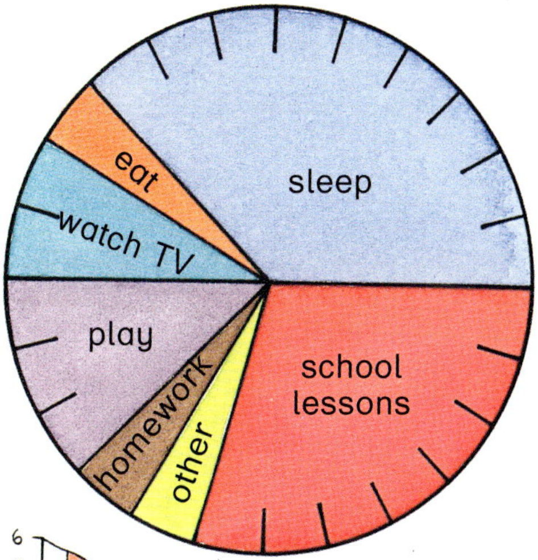

What fraction of the day did Frances spend:

1 sleeping?

2 eating?

3 at school lessons?

4 Name three activities that together took up exactly 50% of the day.

5 Name three activities that together took up exactly 25% of the day.

6 List the activities. By each one, write how many hours Frances spent on it. Make a bar graph to show these results.

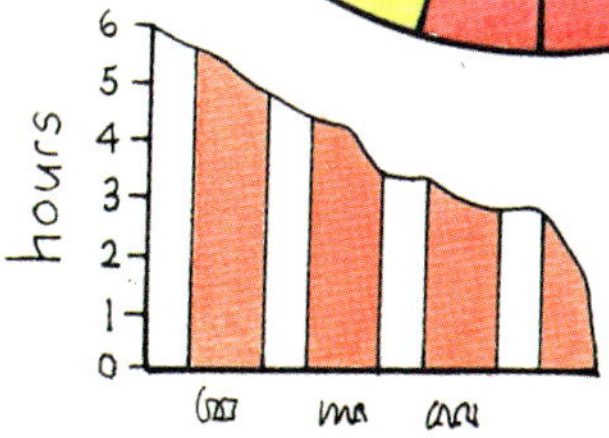

7 Make a pie chart to show how you spend your day. Your activity headings might be different to those of Frances.

To draw your pie chart, draw a circle with the same radius as this circle (4 cm) and trace the divisions on the circumference.

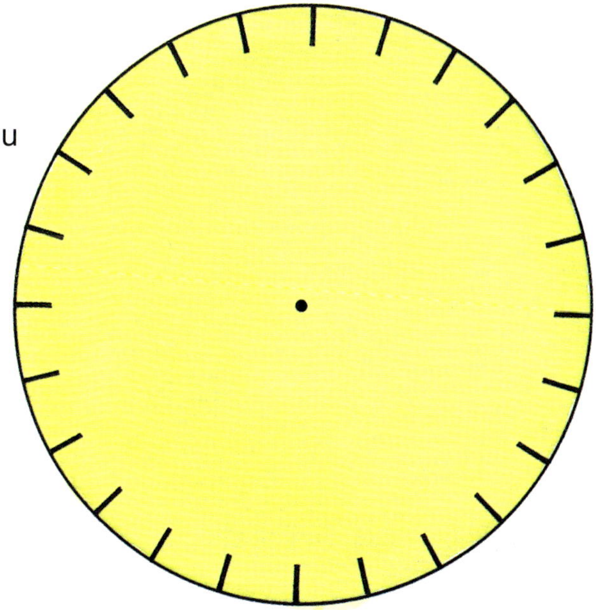

Unit 17 3-D Shape

Octahedron

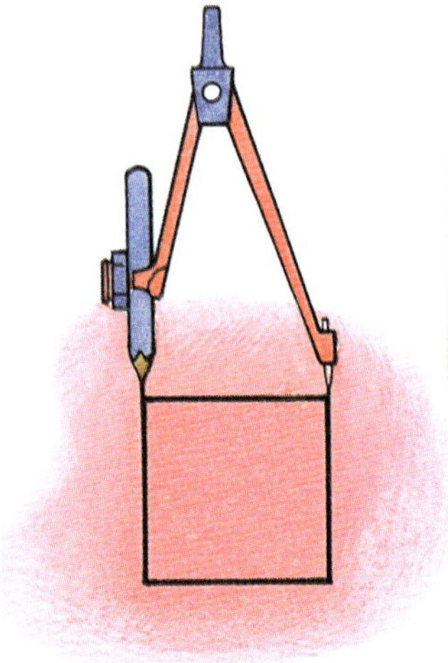

you need:
thin card
ruler
compasses
scissors
Sellotape
glue

You can make a regular octahedron by joining two square-based pyramids.

On thin card, draw a square any size.

Open your compasses to the length of one side.

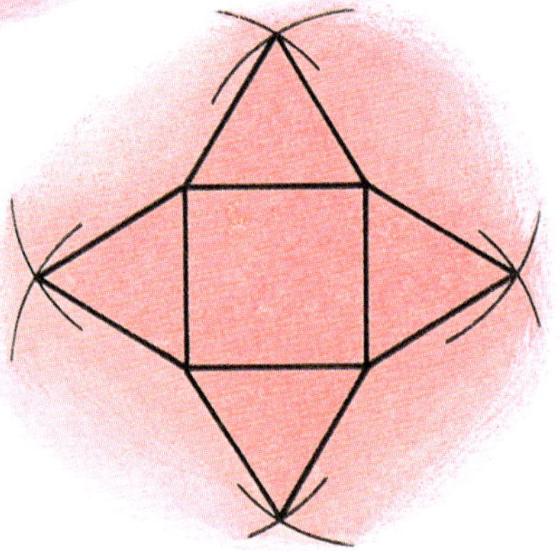

Put the compass point on each vertex of the square in turn and draw arcs that cross.

Join the vertices to where the arcs cross.

This is the net of a square-based pyramid.

Cut out the net, score and fold.

Join the edges with Sellotape.

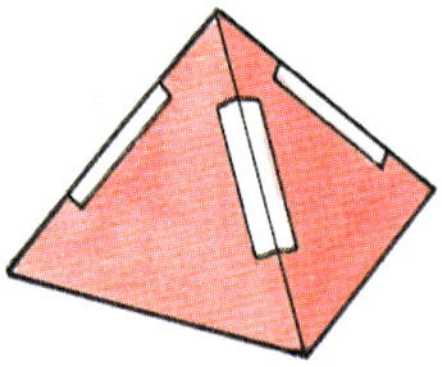

Now make an identical square-based pyramid.
Glue the bases of the two pyramids together to make a regular octahedron.

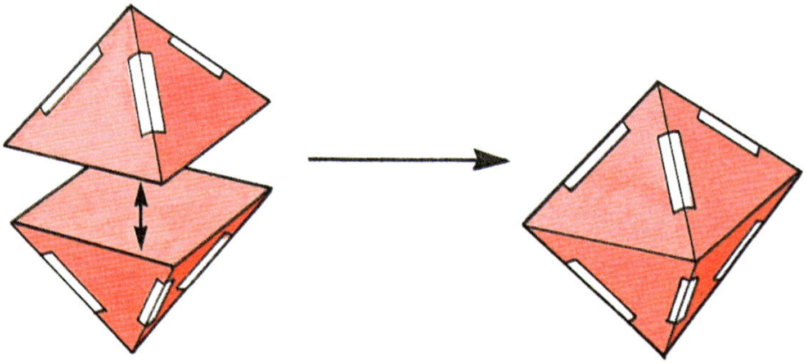

How many faces, vertices and edges does a regular octahedron have?

An unusual 3-D shape

you need:
triangular paper or regular hexagon tiles
scissors
glue
card

This shape is a **truncated tetrahedron**.

This means a tetrahedron with parts sliced off.

tetrahedron

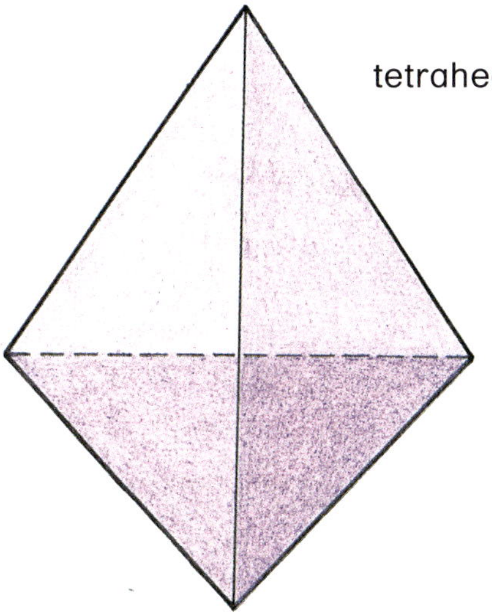

truncated tetrahedron

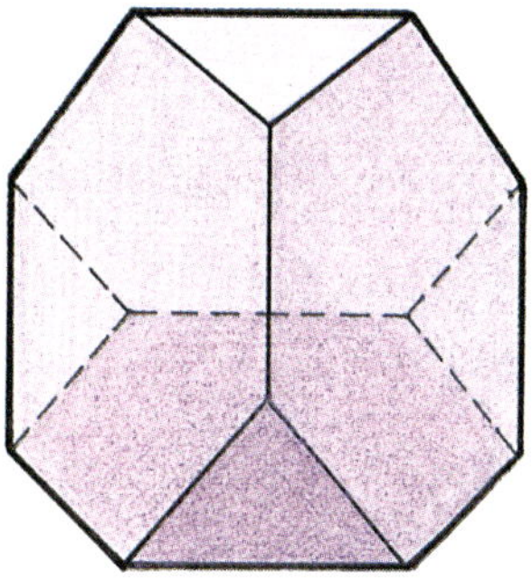

Make a truncated tetrahedron from this net.

You could draw the net on triangular paper or you could draw around shape tiles.

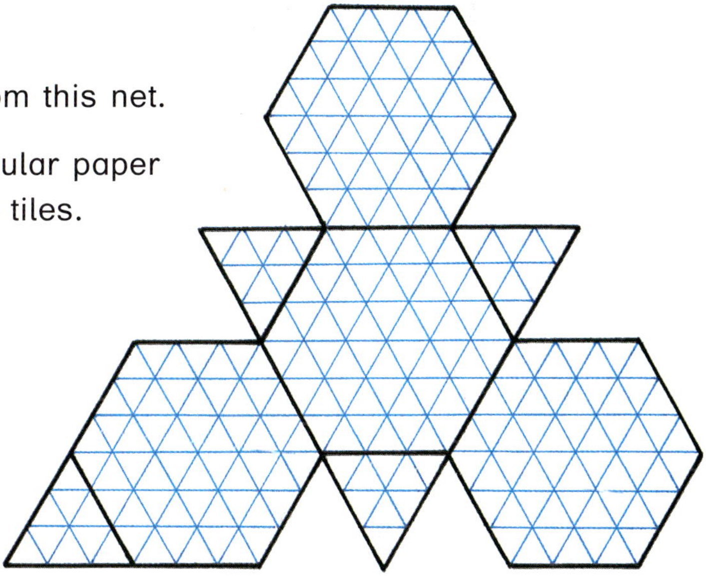

1 Which parts of the tetrahedron have been 'sliced off'?

2 How many faces, vertices and edges does a truncated tetrahedron have? Compare these numbers with the numbers for an ordinary tetrahedron.

Unit 18 Metric – Imperial Conversions

Ginger biscuits

John is going to make ginger biscuits. Here are the ingredients.

12 oz plain flour, $\frac{1}{2}$ oz ground ginger, 1 teaspoon bicarbonate of soda, 6 oz sugar, 5 oz margarine, 1 egg, 3 tablespoons golden syrup

Approximately how many grams of each of these does John need?

1 flour
2 ground ginger
3 sugar
4 margarine

1 oz approx. 25 grams

John goes shopping for some of the ingredients.
Write approximately how many pounds (lb) each item weighs.

1 kg approx. 2 lb

5 

6 

7 

8 

Write approximately how many litres each bucket holds.

1 gallon approx. 4·5 litres

9 

10 

11 

12 

13 Copy this sign, but write the distances in miles.

8 km approx. 5 miles

Parcel post

1 kg approx. 2 lb

1 oz approx. 25 g

8 km approx. 5 miles

Which parcel in each pair is heavier?

1 

2 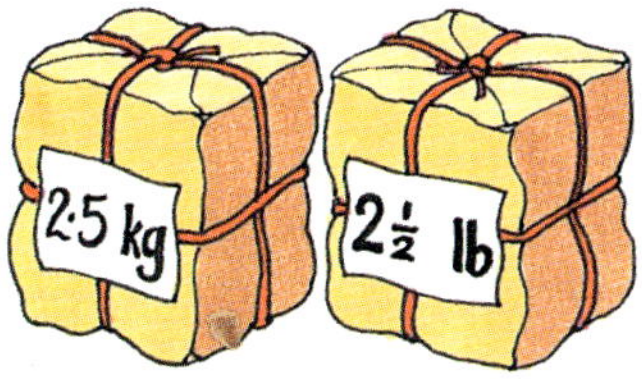

3 

4 Write the weights of these parcels in order, lightest first:

5 Which set of parcels is heavier?

6 Whose route is longer?

Postman Pete's

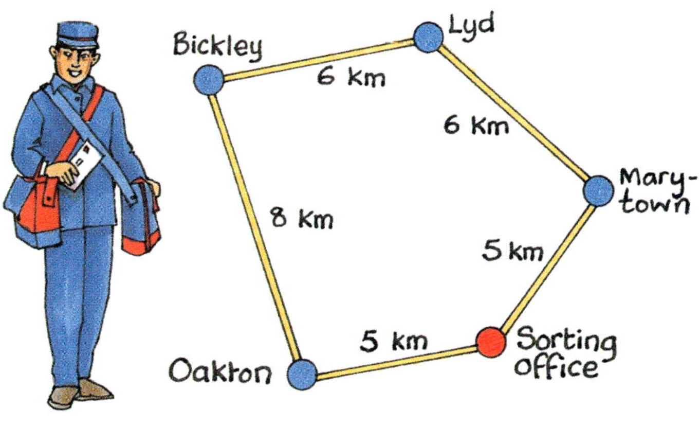

Postwoman Pam's

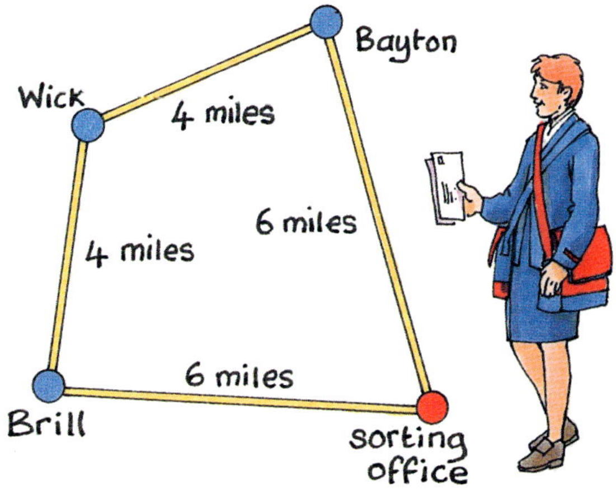

Acknowledgements

The authors and publisher would like to thank the following for their valuable contributions to **maths 2000** at this level:

Reviewers
Rae Cook
Morag Cunningham
June Gemmell
Heather Gray
Fionna Kent
Marion Lewis
Pat MacConnacher
Vivienne Mulholland
Elizabeth Stevenson

Illustrators
Wendy Hesse
Margaret Jones
Martin Orme
Jeffrey Reid
Fran Sewell
Pamela Venus

Photography
Jack Pollard, Studio 15
Images Colour Library
Planet Earth Pictures
Superstock

The authors and publisher are grateful to **NES Arnold** and **Philip & Tacey** for kindly supplying mathematical equipment for inclusion in photographs appearing in the pupils' books.